A MONTH OF
SUNDAYS

A MONTH OF
SUNDAYS

31 Meditations on Resting in God

Glenda Mathes

Reformation Heritage Books
Grand Rapids, Michigan

A Month of Sundays
© 2012 Glenda Mathes

Reformation Heritage Books
2965 Leonard St. NE
Grand Rapids, MI 49525
616-977-0889 / Fax 616-285-3246
orders@heritagebooks.org
www.heritagebooks.org

Printed in the United States of America
12 13 14 15 16 17/10 9 8 7 6 5 4 3 2 1

Library of Congress Cataloging-in-Publication Data

Mathes, Glenda.
  A month of Sundays : 31 meditations on resting in God / Glenda Mathes.
    p. cm.
  ISBN 978-1-60178-194-9 (pbk.)
  1. Bible—Meditations. I. Title.
  BS491.5.M35 2012
  242'.2—dc23
                                        2012037492

For additional Reformed literature, request a free book list from Reformation Heritage Books at the above regular or e-mail address.

CONTENTS

INTRODUCTION

Rest in the LORD....
—PSALM 37:7a

The concept of rest permeates the Bible from creation to consummation. After God created and named the different aspects of our universe in six days, He rested. When Christ returns to complete His kingdom, all believers will enjoy perfect rest. Between these two great bookends of history, God calls us to rest in Him every day.

In today's hectic and distressing world, we need to recapture the concept of daily rest. Demands and distractions agitate our spirits. Disasters trigger anxiety. Diseases generate pain. Despair creeps into our hearts. These influences displace our peace and pull us from resting in God and His Word. The reflections in *A Month of Sundays: 31 Meditations on Resting in God* pause our spinning thoughts and calm our fluctuating feelings.

Real rest is impossible apart from belief in the triune God. In his *Confessions,* Augustine of Hippo famously wrote, "Thou movest us to delight in praising Thee; for Thou hast formed us for Thyself, and our hearts are restless till they find rest in Thee." God created people to praise Him. We are inherently restless apart from saving faith in this Creator God. God instituted the Sabbath as a creation ordinance.

We must set aside one day each week for worship and rest. But true Sabbath keeping includes an attitude of worship and rest that He calls us to develop daily.

Psalm 37:7 commands us: "Rest in the LORD." In Jeremiah 6:16, God says, "Stand ye in the ways, and see, and ask for the old paths, where is the good way, and walk therein, and ye shall find rest for your souls." These verses refer to more than mere Sunday worship. Our souls find rest when we truly trust a sovereign God, who is also our loving Father, and walk in His ways every day of our lives. True rest begins with faith in His Son, our Savior, Jesus Christ. It continues when we reject sin and embrace sanctification through the Holy Spirit.

The Heidelberg Catechism beautifully expounds on the complementary concepts of Sabbath rest. As question 103 explores God's will for us in the fourth commandment, its comprehensive answer embraces support for the gospel ministry and an all-encompassing participation in worship on Sunday, which it calls "the festive day of rest." But the answer additionally notes "that every day of my life I rest from my evil ways, let the Lord work in me through his Spirit, and so begin already in this life the eternal Sabbath."

While we worship and rest on Sunday, we must also rest daily by trusting our triune God and obeying His timeless Word. Each of these devotions helps readers do that through a recommended Scripture reading reference, a focus verse (or verses), a meditation, and questions aimed at stimulating personal reflection. May God bless your study of His Word as you pause to enjoy His gift of daily rest while you anticipate His guarantee of eternal rest.

GOD RESTED

1

Read: Genesis 2

And on the seventh day God ended his work which he had made; and he rested on the seventh day from all his work which he had made. And God blessed the seventh day, and sanctified it: because that in it he had rested from all his work which God created and made.

—GENESIS 2:2–3

During each of the six days of creation, God called some thing into being by the power of His spoken word, and then He named it. Time began and order was established. Each thing did exactly what it was created to do. Light passed into night. Puffy clouds floated in blue sky above a rippling sea. Fruit ripened on supple tree branches. Plump heads of grain undulated in gentle breezes. The sun's golden globe daily bathed the earth with its warm rays. The moon's silver disc nightly shimmered among millions of sparkling stars. Squawking gulls skimmed past spurting whales. Deer grazed fearlessly beside calm lakes. In this perfect creation, Adam and Eve reigned as God's regents.

On the seventh day, God rested. Since God's strength never ebbs, He didn't need to rest. But He chose to cease work for an entire day and, in fellowship within the triune Godhead and with His creatures, enjoy His very good creation.

God blessed and sanctified the seventh day, making it holy. He established a Sabbath pattern for us by setting one day apart from the others as a special day for rejuvenating worship and joyful rest. Even though Christ's resurrection generated the Christian observance on the first day of the week, Sabbath remains a creation ordinance. God confirmed this decree in the fourth commandment, which is the longest of the Ten Commandments:

> Remember the sabbath day, to keep it holy. Six days shalt thou labour, and do all thy work: but the seventh day is the sabbath of the LORD thy God: in it thou shalt not do any work, thou, nor thy son, nor thy daughter, thy manservant, nor thy maidservant, nor thy cattle, nor thy stranger that is within thy gates: for in six days the LORD made heaven and earth, the sea, and all that in them is, and rested the seventh day: wherefore the LORD blessed the sabbath day, and hallowed it (Ex. 20:8–11).

Exodus 20 clearly connects God's rest on the seventh day of creation week with our Sabbath rest each week. On Sunday, we rest from our regular work and gather with other believers to worship God corporately. But remembering the Sabbath day and keeping it holy encompasses much more than merely making time for formal worship.

Notice with what event God links the fourth commandment in Deuteronomy 5: "And remember that thou wast a servant in the land of Egypt, and that the LORD thy God brought thee out thence through a mighty hand and by a stretched out arm: therefore the LORD thy God commanded thee to keep the sabbath day (Deut. 5:15). Here God ties Sabbath observance with His amazing deliverance of the Israelite nation from Egyptian oppression. Just as

God brought Israel out of bondage to Pharaoh, He delivers believers from slavery to sin. Sabbath rest includes not only an appropriate view of the Lord's Day but also a daily turning from sin and submission to the Spirit.

The Heidelberg Catechism elaborates on the comprehensive character of Sabbath keeping while tying together the complementary concepts of Sunday rest and daily rest. Exploring God's will for us in the fourth commandment, the answer to question 103 states:

> First, that the gospel ministry and education for it be maintained, and that, especially on the festive day of rest, I regularly attend the assembly of God's people to learn what God's Word teaches, to participate in the sacraments, to pray to God publicly, and to bring Christian offerings for the poor. Second, that every day of my life I rest from my evil ways, let the Lord work in me through his Spirit, and so begin already in this life the eternal Sabbath.

What lovely language the catechism uses in this inclusive answer!

Note first that the catechism calls Sunday the "festive day of rest." This phrase seems to incorporate two opposing attitudes. We tend to think of "festive" as describing something lively and noisy, like a party or parade. And we tend to think of "rest" as something quiet and sedate, like a nap or coffee break. Considering Sunday as a "festive day of rest" changes how we view and observe it.

Perhaps you grew up with a negative view of Sunday. Legalistic parents can make Sunday observance into a long list of forbidden activities. How much better to focus positively on the unique privileges of a day for corporate worship and personal rest! Thinking of Sunday as a festive day of rest conveys both celebration and peace.

Before question and answer 103 describes Sunday in this colorful way, or even discusses worship, it addresses the gospel ministry in general. Keeping the Sabbath covers a wide variety of things involved in assuring continued corporate worship. We need to encourage, pray for, and financially support our pastors. Those who proclaim the gospel should make their living by the gospel (1 Cor. 9:14). We should also pray for and support those seminaries that train godly ministers.

Appropriate corporate worship encompasses more than simply showing up for every service. Meaningful attendance goes beyond a pew-parked body to include an open mind and a teachable spirit. Worship in Spirit and truth incorporates recognizing and repenting from personal sin. Appropriate worship overflows with gratitude for Christ's sacrifice while joyfully celebrating and jointly praying with other believers. It embraces cheerful giving for others' benefit, not for the tax break.

The second part of question 103's answer shares this book's focus. God calls us to rest daily from sin by obeying the Lord's commands and the Spirit's leading. As the Holy Spirit works in our hearts, we enjoy the beginning of the eternal Sabbath rest God has prepared for us.

God set the Sabbath rest pattern when He rested from His creation work on the seventh day. He calls us to follow that pattern every Sunday, and He calls us to rest in Him every day. We'll explore biblical guidelines for daily rest in this *Month of Sundays*. Sabbath is a day *and* an attitude.

Questions for Reflection

How does God's resting on the seventh day affect the way I view Sunday?

How does viewing Sunday as a "festive day of rest" color my Sabbath observance?

In what specific ways can I demonstrate an attitude of Sabbath rest today?

2

COVENANTAL CONSOLATION

Read: Genesis 15; 26:1–5, 12–33

After these things the word of the LORD came unto Abram in a vision, saying, Fear not, Abram: I am thy shield, and thy exceeding great reward.
—GENESIS 15:1

And the LORD appeared unto [Isaac] the same night, and said, I am the God of Abraham thy father: fear not, for I am with thee, and will bless thee, and multiply thy seed for my servant Abraham's sake.
—GENESIS 26:24

God deals with His people within the context of His covenant. After Adam, as our covenantal representative, fell into sin, God provided redemption for His children through the promise of a Redeemer. God's initial promise, known as the "mother promise," appears in His words to the serpent after the fall in Genesis 3:15: "And I will put enmity between thee and the woman, and between thy seed and her seed; it shall bruise thy head, and thou shalt bruise his heel."

This marked the beginning of a cosmic conflict that still rages, the antithesis between believers and unbelievers. In the course of that great conflict, Satan would be permitted to bruise the heel of the woman's seed. But the seed of the woman, the promised Redeemer, would bruise Satan's head.

When Adam fell, we all became God's enemies. In His covenantal mercy, however, God provided a way for us to become reconciled to Him. That way is Christ.

In Genesis 15, we see how God chose Abram (who would later be called Abraham) to become the father of a particular people, the line of promise through which Christ would come into the world. Genesis 26 depicts the continuation of God's covenantal promise to Abraham's son Isaac and succeeding generations. This promise is not limited to physical descendants of Abraham, but includes all his spiritual children. Galatians 3:29 says, "And if ye be Christ's, then are ye Abraham's seed, and heirs according to the promise." True Christians continue today as part of God's covenant family.

It is crucial to read Scripture as a unified whole, structured around the overarching theme of God's covenant with His people, coming to expression in the person and work of Christ. Within the context of God's covenantal promises, believers are able to trust God and rest daily in His Spirit. Today's verses focus on God's consolation.

God says to Abram in Genesis 15:1, "Fear not, Abram: I am thy shield, and thy exceeding great reward." God echoes that promise to Abraham's son Isaac in Genesis 26:24 when He says, "Fear not, for I am with thee, and will bless thee, and multiply thy seed for my servant Abraham's sake."

What would you guess is the most common command in the Bible? Perhaps you grew up thinking it was the command to obey authority. Or perhaps you believe it is the command to love. These are important and frequent commands, but God most often tells believers, "Fear not."

In today's verses, God connects the command to fear not with assurances that He is with His covenant people. He was with Adam and Eve in the garden. After they ruptured the sweetness and intimacy of their original communion with God, He mercifully came to them, covered their nakedness, and provided a plan of redemption.

God was with Abraham. He promised to be his shield and his exceeding great reward. God not only protects His people, but He also abundantly blesses them.

God was with Isaac. He reminded him of His covenantal relationship with his father, Abraham. He promised to bless Isaac and multiply his descendants for the sake of Abraham, whom He called "my servant."

Was Abraham God's servant because he lived a perfect life? Hardly! Read Genesis 12:10–20, 16, and 20 to get a glimpse of the ways Abraham failed to trust and rest in God's promises. But Galatians 3, the same chapter stating that today's believers belong to God's covenant as Abraham's spiritual children, says, "Abraham believed God, and it was accounted to him for righteousness" (v. 6). When Hebrews 11 lists believers in what is sometimes called "the hall of faith," Abraham is discussed more than any others. That chapter describes faith as "the substance of things hoped for, the evidence of things not seen" (v. 1). It concisely overviews covenant history by showing how believers are counted faithful despite their doubts and transgressions. By working faith in believers' hearts, the Spirit enables ordinary people to do extraordinary things. We are God's servants when we serve Him through faith in Christ and the equipping of the Spirit.

God blesses His people and deals with them and their families within the context of covenant community. Because God is always with us, dealing with us in His covenantal love, because He has provided a way of salvation through the finished work of Jesus Christ, and because the Spirit equips us, we are able to fear not. We rest in God.

In what may well be the most beautiful expression of confessional comfort, Lord's Day 1 of the Heidelberg Catechism exemplifies why believers can face life without fear:

Q. What is your only comfort in life and in death?

A. That I am not my own, but belong—body and soul, in life and in death—to my faithful Savior Jesus Christ. He has fully paid for all my sins with his precious blood, and has set me free from the tyranny of the devil. He also watches over me in such a way that not a hair can fall from my head without the will of my Father in heaven: in fact, all things must work together for my salvation. Because I belong to him, Christ, by his Holy Spirit, assures me of eternal life and makes me whole-heartedly willing and ready from now on to live for him.

How amazing that this confession conveys God's comfort in such lovely and biblical language! No wonder so many people memorize and treasure these words. May God's covenantal promises in Christ become real to you as you rest in His Spirit.

Questions for Reflection

How do God's covenantal promises console me?

How have I seen God fulfill the biblical promises of Lord's Day 1 in my life?

In what specific ways can I rest today in the joy of God's consolation?

3

TEN COMFORTS

Read: Exodus 20

And Moses said unto the people, Fear not: for God is come to prove you, and that his fear may be before your faces, that ye sin not.
—EXODUS 20:20

When you read Exodus 20, are you surprised at seeing the command to fear not in the same chapter as the Ten Commandments? Is Moses' command in verse 20 to "fear not" contradictory when in the same sentence he encourages fear? Although the placement or use of the word "fear" may initially seem illogical, it was not illogical for the Israelites then, and it is not for us now.

The Israelites had good reason to be afraid. Smoke billowed from the mountain. Lightning blazed across the sky. Thunderclaps and trumpet blasts assaulted their ears. They knew what God could do. They had seen Him change water into blood as well as other amazing miracles during the ten plagues in Egypt. They had seen God lead them with pillars of cloud and fire. They had walked through towering walls of water—walls that crashed down on Pharaoh's host, drowning and sweeping them away. Bread rained from heaven, water gushed from a rock, and the sun stood still. Small wonder they trembled when Moses warned they would die if they came too close to the smoking mountain!

God could, indeed, strike dead any who disobeyed. But Moses assured the people that they didn't need to be afraid. God had come to prove or test them. He wanted the Israelites to realize His power and perfection because keeping that awareness in the forefront of their minds would help them resist sin.

While the biblical command to fear God includes recognizing His might and holiness, it does not mean trembling before Him in abject terror. Fearing God is a comprehensive concept that includes a healthy awe and reverence as well as a heartfelt love and desire to obey Him. Like little children, we believe our Father can do anything and is always right. We know He is capable of administering painful discipline; however, we want to obey Him—not from fear of punishment—but because we love Him so much.

Obedience as gratitude colors the way we view the Ten Commandments. We don't obey them simply to avoid destruction. We obey them because we love our heavenly Father and want to please Him. When we see the Ten Commandments as guidelines for gratitude, we begin to see how fearing God complements the comfort of fearing not. Our grateful comfort grows when we realize that we cannot keep God's law and when we consider how Christ willingly obeyed God's law in our place.

The Ten Commandments guide our relationships with God and our neighbors. Jesus summed up the law:

> And thou shalt love the Lord thy God with all thy heart, and with all thy soul, and with all thy mind, and with all thy strength: this is the first commandment. And the

second is like, namely this, Thou shalt love thy neighbour as thyself. There is none other commandment greater than these (Mark 12:30–31).

Christ's summary is convicting. No one can love God and neighbor fully at any given moment, let alone all the time. We all fall far short.

This realization of our failure is another way the Ten Commandments guide us. They bring us to repentance by awakening an awareness of our sin. Paul wrote, "Therefore by the deeds of the law there shall no flesh be justified in his sight: for by the law is the knowledge of sin" (Rom. 3:20).

The law shows us our sin, but obeying the law does not save us. Paul wrote that "no flesh" shall be justified by doing the deeds of the law. If we are not justified by obeying the law, is there no hope? On the contrary—we have great hope! And our hope is not in ourselves, but in Christ. What a comfort!

We take comfort in knowing that Christ's perfect obedience throughout His life and in His death fulfilled the demands of God's law. Christ Himself declared, "Think not that I am come to destroy the law, or the prophets: I am not come to destroy, but to fulfil" (Matt. 5:17).

Christ came, not to banish God's law or ignore it, but to complete it. We can't obey God's law perfectly, but Christ could, and He did. Truly God and truly man, He came to earth as our mediator. He reconciled us to God and restored us to fellowship with Him. Our Lord Jesus Christ lived an obedient life and died an atoning death. He did all the things we should have done, and He died for all the things we should not have done.

If you trust Christ for your salvation, you do not need to fear your heavenly Father. Your only fear of Him can be an awe-filled reverence and wholehearted love. You no longer need to feel anxious that your failures to perfectly obey God's Ten Commandments will incur His eternal wrath. Instead, you can thank God for His great gift of salvation through Jesus Christ. Finding your comfort in Christ's completed work, you can now obey the Ten Commandments through the Spirit's power in gratitude for your salvation.

Obedience doesn't earn salvation, but it evidences gratitude. Disobedience impairs Sabbath rest and daily rest. Belief in Christ and trust in God the Father generate rest through the Spirit's work in our hearts. The triune God comforts us with the knowledge that Christ has perfectly fulfilled every word of the law. We rest in the Lord.

Knowing God's holiness and power, we fear Him with awe and reverence. Loving Him as our dear heavenly Father, we obey Him out of gratitude. God's commandments guide our relationships with God and our neighbors. Through Christ's atoning work and the equipping of the Spirit, the Ten Commandments become our ten comforts.

Questions for Reflection

How does the biblical concept of fearing God change the way I'll pray and live today?

In what ways do I live as if obedience contributes to my salvation?

In what ways can I rest in the Ten Commandments as ten comforts?

4

GOOD COURAGE

Read: Deuteronomy 31 and Joshua 1

Be strong and of a good courage, fear not, nor be afraid of them: for the LORD thy God, he it is that doth go with thee; he will not fail thee, nor forsake thee.
—DEUTERONOMY 31:6

Have I not commanded thee? Be strong and of a good courage; be not afraid, neither be thou dismayed: for the LORD thy God is with thee whithersoever thou goest.
—JOSHUA 1:9

The book of Deuteronomy dawns with the Israelites on the threshold of the Promised Land. Moses reminded them that their disobedience had led to an extra forty years of wandering in the wilderness. He reviewed the Ten Commandments in Deuteronomy 5, renewing God's covenant with His people. He recited additional history and listed more detailed rules for living as God's people in their own land. Since Moses failed to trust God and disobeyed Him by striking a rock for water when he was commanded only to speak to it, he was not permitted to enter the land. Deuteronomy concludes as he prepares to hand the reins of leadership to Joshua.

Moses bookended his instructions to Israel with similar exhortations about trusting in God. In Deuteronomy 1:21, he said, "Behold, the LORD thy God hath set the land before thee: go up and possess it, as the LORD God of thy fathers hath said unto thee; fear not, neither be discouraged." And in Deuteronomy 31:8 he said, "And the LORD, he it is that doth go before thee; he will be with thee, he will not fail thee, neither forsake thee: fear not, neither be dismayed."

As one of the only two fighting men that God had allowed to live through the entire wilderness journey, Joshua had many opportunities to learn from Moses' example and teaching. An apt pupil, Joshua learned his lessons well. When he prepared the Israelites to take the land, he encouraged them by reiterating Moses' final command to "be strong and of a good courage" (Josh. 1:9). Later, he would tell his military leaders, "Fear not, nor be dismayed, be strong and of good courage" (Josh. 10:25).

All this might suggest, at first glance, that if believers are strong or courageous enough they will never be afraid, dismayed, or discouraged. But don't miss the emphasis on the Lord's continued presence. He goes with us, never fails us, and never forsakes us. It is only in the Lord that weak believers can be strong. We don't draw courage from ourselves and our abilities. Only God gives us good courage.

The people of Israel saw God's power demonstrated in an amazing way as they obeyed God's strange commands for Jericho's conquest. What military strategist would advocate marching around a city for days? But that is what the Israelite army did. Soldiers solemnly marched before seven trumpet-blowing priests and the ark of the covenant, which was followed by the rear guard. The entire procession walked around the city once on each of six successive days. Can you imagine how strange this tactic looked? Even if the people in the city were frightened on the first day, they were surely hooting in derision by the sixth day.

The plan changed, however, on the seventh day. Instead of walking around Jericho only once, the procession circled the city seven times. Perhaps Jericho's inhabitants began to wonder what was happening during the second or third circuit. The tension must have mounted by the seventh time. An eerie stillness may have filled the city as its people looked over the walls or listened apprehensively within. Breaking the suspenseful silence, the priests blew a loud trumpet blast and the Israelites shouted. The impressive ramparts of Jericho immediately collapsed. The city literally fell into the Israelites' hands with almost no effort on their part. It's difficult to imagine a more effective demonstration of God's power.

We don't have to trust in our own physical strength or mental acumen. We don't have to trust in a capable president or a powerful military. We must simply trust our mighty God. When we need it, He gives us good courage.

Later, the Israelites were disheartened by a painful defeat at the hands of men from the city of Ai and were understandably reluctant to attack Ai again. God Himself appeared to Joshua and told him, "Fear not, neither be thou dismayed" (Josh. 8:1).

In these verses from Deuteronomy and Joshua, we read God's command to be strong and courageous combined with the common exhortation to fear not. But we also see God promising never to leave us or forsake us. That refrain of God's constant care resounds again and again throughout Scripture.

David echoes today's texts when he presents his son Solomon with plans and materials for building the temple of God in Jerusalem:

> Be strong and of good courage, and do it: fear not, nor
> be dismayed: for the LORD God, even my God, will be
> with thee; he will not fail thee, nor forsake thee, until
> thou hast finished all the work for the service of the
> house of the LORD (1 Chron. 28:20).

David wrote this long before advertisers promoted the
Nike brand with its "Just do it!" slogan. But he says basi-
cally the same thing. Because God will be with Solomon, he
shouldn't hesitate to begin. He doesn't need to be dismayed
by the immensity of the mammoth project he faces. God
will guide his every step and will carry the work through to
completion. In God's strength, he can be strong. God will
grant him good courage.

God's promise never to leave or forsake us is also found
in the New Testament. After Christ's resurrection and
prior to His ascension, Christ confirms this promise to
the church in the words of what has become known as the
Great Commission:

> And Jesus came and spake unto them, saying, All power
> is given unto me in heaven and in earth. Go ye there-
> fore, and teach all nations, baptizing them in the name
> of the Father, and of the Son, and of the Holy Ghost:
> teaching them to observe all things whatsoever I have
> commanded you: and, lo, I am with you always, even
> unto the end of the world. Amen (Matt. 28:18–20).

Because Christ reigns at the right hand of God and has
complete authority over the entire cosmos, believers can
spread the gospel throughout the world. New believers are
to be baptized in the name of the triune God, but they are
also to be taught. We must teach them to obey everything
God has commanded in His Word. This daunting task is

possible because our Lord is with us always, even unto the very end of time.

Christ is always with us. For that reason, we can spread the gospel far and wide, teaching the whole truth of God's Word. We can face the Jerichos in our lives, even that last enemy death, because we can be sure that God will give His people good courage.

Questions for Reflection

How does the Great Commission impact the way I live my life daily?

How is my obedience connected to courage?

In what ways do I need to depend more on the Lord and rest in Him for my good courage today?

REDEEMING LOVE

5

Read: Ruth 4

*And the women said unto Naomi, Blessed be the LORD,
which hath not left thee this day without a kinsman, that his
name may be famous in Israel. And he shall be unto thee a
restorer of thy life, and a nourisher of thine old age: for thy
daughter in law, which loveth thee, which is better to thee
than seven sons, hath born him.*
— RUTH 4:14–15

No other book in the Bible reads as much like a literary
novel as the book of Ruth. Cliff-hangers propel the action
forward. Believable characters demonstrate personality progression. And who doesn't enjoy a well-written love story?
But this love story isn't simply about feelings between Ruth
and Boaz. It isn't even about how Naomi finds fulfillment.
This story is all about God's love for His people and His
plan of redemption.

Backstory at the beginning of the book tells us that these
events took place during the sad time when judges ruled
Israel, an era characterized by this refrain: "In those days
there was no king in Israel: every man did that which was
right in his own eyes" (Judg. 21:25). The reader also learns
that a famine led an Israelite family to leave Bethlehem in
Judah to live in Moab.

Like any good novel, this story provides a prompt introduction of conflict. People of the promised line, living in the Promised Land, should be trusting God's promises. Instead, this family moves to a foreign land, where the father dies. After marrying foreign women, the sons also die. When the widow, Naomi, hears that the famine is over, she decides to return to her own land. The primary narrative begins.

While rest is an underlying theme in Ruth, a few references directly address it. The first occurs when Naomi urged her daughters-in-law, Orpah and Ruth, to turn back from accompanying her and return to their mothers in the hope of finding new husbands: "The LORD grant you that ye may find rest, each of you in the house of her husband. Then she kissed them; and they lifted up their voice, and wept" (1:9).

The rest Naomi speaks of here doesn't mean inactivity, but rather security. In that culture and time, a widow had little hope for protection and a future. A woman needed a husband to care for her present welfare and sons to secure her future well-being.

Orpah chose to return to Moab, but Ruth clung to Naomi, confessing her loyalty in words frequently used at modern weddings:

> Intreat me not to leave thee, or to return from following after thee: for whither thou goest, I will go; and where thou lodgest, I will lodge: thy people shall be my people, and thy God my God: where thou diest, will I die, and there will I be buried: the LORD do so to me, and more also, if ought but death part thee and me (1:16–17).

Ruth's speech expressed more than mere sentiments of devotion. She turned her back on her national gods and confessed belief in the covenant God. She rejected her native land and embraced the Promised Land. And she called upon God as her witness that she meant every word she said. Her allegiances had been changed by God's Spirit.

When Naomi and Ruth arrived in Bethlehem, the women of the city greeted them. Naomi spoke of herself as "empty," saying that the Almighty had bitterly afflicted her (1:20–21). The reader's interest is piqued as the chapter ends with this cliff-hanger: "and they came to Bethlehem in the beginning of barley harvest" (1:22).

The story of God's providence unfolds. Gleaning for grain, Ruth "just happened" to work in a field owned by Boaz, a wealthy relative of her late husband. Having heard of her kindness to Naomi and changed loyalties, he said to her, "The LORD recompense thy work, and a full reward be given thee of the LORD God of Israel, under whose wings thou art come to trust" (2:12). He urged her to continue gleaning with his maidservants under his protection. He allowed her to eat and drink with his harvesters. He even told his young men to leave extra grain for her as they bound the sheaves.

Was Boaz kind to Ruth because of the good report he had heard about her? Was affection for her already stirring in his heart? Perhaps he had a special attraction to her because his own mother was a foreigner, the former prostitute Rahab (Matt. 1:5). Whatever human reasons we might see behind his kindness, Boaz was moved by God's Spirit to compassion for His own redemptive purpose: the progression of the promised line. Amazed at the amount of grain Ruth brings home, Naomi is pleased when she hears that the generous farmer is Boaz. The plot thickens.

The third chapter begins and ends with intriguing references to rest. Naomi sought to ensure a future for herself and Ruth by securing the protection of a kinsman redeemer: "Then Naomi her mother in law said unto her, My daughter, shall I not seek rest for thee, that it may be well with thee?" (3:1).

Naomi wasn't concerned with romance, but with rest. She wanted Ruth to marry a relative who could function as a redeemer, continuing the family line while providing comfort and protection. The kinsman redeemer was a picture of the great Redeemer.

Since Boaz was a likely candidate for a kinsman redeemer, Naomi coached Ruth in an effort to secure his permanent protection through marriage. The women's endeavors appeared to be taking effect. Naomi believed Boaz would soon act: "Then said she, Sit still, my daughter, until thou know how the matter will fall: for the man will not be in rest, until he have finished the thing this day" (3:18).

Boaz felt compelled to act. Since he was an older man (3:10), still unmarried, he may not have been impulsive; however, God's Spirit urged him forward. Boaz arranged for the redemption of Naomi's property and marriage to Ruth to perpetuate her dead husband's name. God blessed Boaz and Ruth with the birth of a son, Obed, who would become the grandfather of David in the promised line of the Messiah. The women who greeted a bitter and empty Naomi now sing praises to God for filling her with the gift of this son, a child who would further the line of promise toward that great child of promise, the ultimate Redeemer who grants His people rest.

In our busy world, we find our rest only in Him. Trust Him to provide for your every need as He did for Ruth. Your loving Redeemer will graciously grant you rest.

Questions for Reflection

Is the book of Ruth simply a love story? Why or why not?

In what ways does Boaz typify Christ?

How can I see God's providence in my life today and rest confidently in it?

6

GOLDEN REST

Read: 1 Kings 8

Blessed be the LORD, that hath given rest unto his people Israel, according to all that he promised: there hath not failed one word of all his good promise, which he promised by the hand of Moses his servant. The LORD our God be with us, as he was with our fathers: let him not leave us, nor forsake us: that he may incline our hearts unto him, to walk in all his ways, and to keep his commandments, and his statutes, and his judgments, which he commanded our fathers.

—1 KINGS 8:56–58

Fast-forward from the birth of Obed when there was no king in Israel, through the reign of his grandson King David, to the golden age of Israel under David's son, Solomon, who built the temple. Solomon's actions and prayer at the temple's dedication are recorded in 1 Kings 8. The focus verses echo the refrain of God's promise never to leave us or forsake us, while reminding us that His promises never fail.

Even though David had desired to build the temple, God did not permit him because he was a man of war. God declared that task would go to David's son: "Behold, a son shall be born to thee, who shall be a man of rest; and I will give him rest from all his enemies round about: for his name shall be Solomon, and I will give peace and quietness unto Israel in his days" (1 Chron. 22:9).

Solomon was a man of rest; even his name calls to mind the Hebrew word for peace: *shalom*. God granted him rest from all his surrounding enemies, ushering in Israel's golden age and the peace necessary to build the temple. Seeking cedars from Hiram, king of Tyre, Solomon sent him a message acknowledging this gift of rest:

> Thou knowest how that David my father could not build a house unto the name of the LORD his God for the wars which were about him on every side, until the LORD put them under the soles of his feet. But now the LORD my God hath given me rest on every side, so that there is neither adversary nor evil occurrent (1 Kings 5:3–4).

King Solomon and the people of Israel enjoyed rest from marauding outlaws and attacking armies. Under God's protection, they lived in safety. Blessed with peace and prosperity, they devoted their full attention to building a temple to glorify the Lord.

A second report of the temple's dedication is found in 2 Chronicles 5–7. Glimpses of the temple's beauty and grandeur can been seen in the descriptions of its materials and workmanship recorded in 1 Kings 5–7 or 2 Chronicles 2–4. The temple was constructed of hewn stones and carved cedars with fir floors and folding doors. Gold gilded the entire house and its furnishings. Cast brass pillars, molded borders, basins, and utensils glinted in the light.

In 1 Kings 8, Solomon's prayer at the temple's dedication shows this was a time of not only physical rest but also spiritual rest. Solomon begins his corporate prayer by adoring the Most High God and praising His covenant care for His people: "And he said, LORD God of Israel, there is no God like thee, in heaven above, or on earth beneath, who keepest covenant and mercy with thy servants that walk before thee with all their heart" (v. 23).

Solomon confessed that God cannot be contained in the entire cosmos, let alone the paltry temple, but that the mighty God condescends to hear the prayer of His servant (vv. 27–28). Reciting a litany of likely trials, Solomon asks God to hear His people's prayers through them all and to forgive their sins. In verses 38–39, he prays not only for forgiveness of corporate sin but also of each person's personal sin:

> What prayer and supplication soever be made by any man, or by all thy people Israel, which shall know every man the plague of his own heart, and spread forth his hands toward this house: then hear thou in heaven thy dwelling place, and forgive, and do, and give to every man according to his ways, whose heart thou knowest; (for thou, even thou only, knowest the hearts of all the children of men).

Solomon recognized the need for personal introspection and repentance. God alone knows our secret sins. These private sins may not be visible to others, but like bacteria or germs, they sicken our souls and cause diseased hearts. He also realized that every individual struggles with sin: "for there is no man that sinneth not" (v. 46). This confirms biblical teaching found in multiple texts such as Psalm 14:3, Psalm 53:3, and Romans 3:10.

Solomon's prayer concludes with a great confession that, like his opening, reminds us of how God's promises never fail and again emphasizes the concept of rest:

> Blessed be the LORD, that hath given rest unto his peo-
> ple Israel, according to all that he promised: there hath
> not failed one word of all his good promise, which he
> promised by the hand of Moses his servant. The LORD
> our God be with us, as he was with our fathers: let him
> not leave us, nor forsake us: that he may incline our
> hearts unto him, to walk in all his ways, and to keep
> his commandments, and his statutes, and his judg-
> ments, which he commanded our fathers. And let these
> my words, wherewith I have made supplication before
> the LORD, be nigh unto the LORD our God day and
> night, that he maintain the cause of his servant, and the
> cause of his people Israel at all times, as the matter shall
> require: that all the people of the earth may know that
> the LORD is God, and that there is none else. Let your
> heart therefore be perfect with the LORD our God, to
> walk in his statures, and to keep his commandments, as
> at this day (vv. 56–61).

Notice again the familiar refrain of God's constant care.
God promises never to leave us or forsake us for a reason:
that He may incline our hearts to Him so that we will walk
in all His ways. And we are to walk in His ways for a reason:
that all the people of the earth may know the Lord is God
and there is no other.

Do you feel as if you wage wars on multiple fronts? Pray
for God to give you rest from your surrounding enemies.
Do you feel lonely and isolated? Remember that God has
promised never to leave you or forsake you. Perhaps so
many people have broken promises to you that you can't
believe this. But believe it! It's true! God never broke one
word of any promises to Israel. He doesn't break any of the
promises He makes to us today. And He will never break

any of His promises to your believing children and grand-children. This is our God! And this is His promise. Walk in His ways today!

Questions for Reflection

How has God given me rest from my surrounding enemies?

Why is it necessary for me to examine my heart today?

In what specific ways can I perform today's tasks to show that I'm walking in God's ways?

7

GREATER ALLIES

Read: 2 Kings 6:8–23

And he answered, Fear not: for they that be with us are more than they that be with them.

—2 KINGS 6:16

Some Old Testament narratives show God's hand in amazing—and even amusing—ways. This story about the invisible army of the Lord makes me smile.

God revealed the king of Syria's movements to Elisha, who faithfully warned the king of Israel, saving him more than once. Elisha so accurately and consistently relayed the plans that the king of Syria believed one of his own servants had betrayed him. When he confronted his servants, one responded (in obvious hyperbole) that Elisha knew even the words the king spoke in his bedroom!

Determined to capture Elisha and put an end to this dissemination of information, the king of Syria sent out a great army, complete with horses and chariots. At night, the Syrian forces encircled the town where Elisha slept. When Elisha's servant woke in the morning and saw the army encompassing the city, he was terrified. Elisha calmed his fears, telling him there were more with them than were with the Syrians, and prayed for the young man's eyes to be opened. Immediately

God revealed an army of fiery horses and chariots covering the slopes of the surrounding mountains.

How often do we feel frightened and surrounded by forces that appear completely overwhelming? But we see only the physical things; we don't see the spiritual realities. Our finite eyesight fails to focus on the Lord's protection and power. Who knows how frequently we're surrounded by a mighty host of angelic allies?

This narrative appears immediately before an account of the amazing way God delivered Samaria from the Syrian army's long siege. God caused the Syrian soldiers to hear what sounded like hundreds of thundering horses and rumbling chariots. Convinced they were under attack from a combined force of neighboring nations, the Syrians abandoned everything in their tents and fled. God's hosts were Israel's greater allies.

Today's focus verse recalls several Old Testament texts and situations. When faced by an overwhelming host of combined armies, Jehoshaphat offered a corporate prayer that reminded the people of God's promises and begged for divine intervention. At the conclusion of his prayer, a godly man prophesied: "And he said, Hearken ye, all Judah, and ye inhabitants of Jerusalem, and thou king Jehoshaphat, Thus saith the LORD unto you, Be not afraid nor dismayed by reason of this great multitude; for the battle is not yours, but God's" (2 Chron. 20:15).

Hear again the familiar refrain: "Be not afraid nor dismayed." Emboldened by faith in God and led by singers praising the Lord, the army went out to meet the threatening hordes. The Jewish soldiers came upon an astonishing scene of slaughter. Bloody corpses testified that the opposing forces had annihilated each other.

A similar scenario unfolded at the time Sennacherib, the Assyrian king, threatened Judah under King Hezekiah. In a relentless push for power, Sennacherib's military might had destroyed every nation in its way. His emissaries threatened the Jewish people, criticized Hezekiah, and blasphemed God.

God intervened. Through the prophet Isaiah, He comforted His people and decreed Sennacherib's demise:

> And Isaiah said unto them, Thus shall ye say to your master, Thus saith the LORD, Be not afraid of the words which thou hast heard, with which the servants of the king of Assyria have blasphemed me. Behold, I will send a blast upon him, and he shall hear a rumour, and shall return to his own land: and I will cause him to fall by the sword in his own land (2 Kings 19:6–7).

Like Jehoshaphat, Hezekiah prayed for deliverance. By God's gracious Spirit, he became bold and told the people:

> Be strong and courageous, be not afraid nor dismayed for the king of Assyria, nor for all the multitude that is with him: for there be more with us than with him: with him is an arm of flesh; but with us is the LORD our God to help us, and to fight our battles. And the people rested themselves upon the words of Hezekiah king of Judah (2 Chronicles 32:7–8).

Here we see familiar and comforting language: "Be not afraid nor dismayed, for there be more with us than with him." We also see that these words enabled the people to put their total trust in God and rest in Him.

That trust was well founded. In one night, the angel of the Lord killed thousands of Assyrian soldiers. Sennacherib returned to Nineveh in humiliation. A short time later, two of his sons slew him while he worshiped his worthless god.

These Old Testament texts assure us that we don't have to be afraid of an enemy host because we have far greater allies. This reminds us of the New Testament text of 1 John 4:4, which warns against the antichristian spirits of the age: "Ye are of God, little children, and have overcome them: because greater is he that is in you, than he that is in the world."

God considers us His own, dear little children. Christ Himself dwells in us, and He is far superior to any worldly physical or unearthly spiritual force. We can be sure of an outcome that glorifies God and promotes the welfare of His children. John so confidently assures us of this that he speaks as if we already have overcome. It's a done deal.

With our limited insight, we fail to see the vast array of God's powerful and protective host. Just as He miraculously delivered His people in the Old Testament, He can still deliver us today. Ask God to give you a calm spirit and enable you to rest in Him. Pray for the ability to look past the physical shadows and see God's eternal realities. When enemies surround you, lift your eyes and witness the hosts of the Lord. There are more with you than with them. Open your eyes to see your greater allies!

Questions for Reflection

In what ways do I feel surrounded?

How do these narratives encourage my heart and give me rest?

What can I do today that will encourage others to see that God is greater than any threat?

RESTFUL PEACE

8

Read: Esther 9

As the days wherein the Jews rested from their enemies, and the month which was turned unto them from sorrow to joy, and from mourning into a good day: that they should make them days of feasting and joy, and of sending portions one to another, and gifts to the poor.

—ESTHER 9:22

Who could imagine that God would use a pagan beauty pageant to save His people from complete annihilation? Yet that is the catalyst God used to place a young Jewish woman in a palace, where she could plead with the king for her people.

The events recorded in Esther take place while the Jews lived in exile. It is famous as the only book in the Bible with no direct mention of God. But God moves behind every event in this narrative, which drips with dramatic irony.

With page-turning suspense, the book tells a story of political intrigue and poetic justice. King Ahasuerus threw a hedonistic "men-only" party and, at the height of his guests' drunkenness, shamelessly demanded that his queen, Vashti, display her beauty before them. Her refusal set into play the book's primary events. Vashti was deposed, and a search for her replacement commenced. Ahasuerus commanded that beautiful young women from throughout the kingdom should be brought into the palace's harem, including the young Jewess who became known as Esther. After a candidate completed a year of beauty treatments, she was brought to spend a night with the king. When Esther's turn came, she pleased King Ahasuerus: "And the king loved Esther above all the women, and she obtained grace and favour in his sight more than all the virgins; so that he set the royal crown upon her head, and made her queen instead of Vashti" (2:17).

Esther's cousin, Mordecai, who had raised her as his daughter, sat at the king's gate, where he refused to bow before the king's right-hand man, Haman. Determined to destroy not only Mordecai but also the entire Jewish population, Haman manipulated the king into decreeing the Jews' complete destruction. Mordecai sent word and a copy of the edict to Esther, telling her to go before the king and plead for her people.

In her reply to Mordecai, Esther told him that anyone who went before the king without being summoned would be put to death, unless the king extended his gold scepter. Esther feared the king's response to her approach since it had been thirty days since he last sent for her. Mordecai urged her to act:

> Then Mordecai commanded to answer Esther, Think not with thyself that thou shalt escape in the king's house, more than all the Jews. For if thou altogether holdest thy peace at this time, then shall there enlargement and deliverance arise to the Jews from another place; but thou and thy father's house shall be destroyed: and who knoweth whether thou art come to the kingdom for such a time as this? (4:13–14).

Esther responded by requesting that Mordecai and all the Jews in the city join her and her maidservants in three days of fasting and prayer. Then, she said, she would go into the king, "which is not according to the law: and if I perish, I perish" (4:16).

God had, indeed, brought Esther into the Sushan citadel for such a time. By God's providence, King Ahasuerus extended his scepter, and Esther lived. Employing extraordinary diplomacy, she invited the king and Haman to a banquet, and then a second one. Meanwhile the story winds in ironic twists, depicting Haman's increasing loss of control under God's supreme sovereignty.

At the second banquet, Esther begged the king to spare her and her people. When the king demanded to know who planned to destroy them, she named Haman as the instigator of the vile plot. After the king stormed into the garden in a rage, Haman threw himself—literally—on Esther, seeking mercy. The king returned to witness what he viewed as Haman's attempt to violate the queen. In unmistakable poetic justice, Haman was hanged on gallows intended for Mordecai.

The arch villain's demise, however, did not ensure the Jews' safety. The previous edict could not be revoked, and the decreed slaughter would occur as scheduled. To prevent a massacre, the king approved a new rule permitting the Jews' self-defense.

On the appointed day, the Jews killed all who sought their lives. God completely inverted the plans of wicked Haman; the Jews became victors instead of victims. Then, God granted His people rest.

Although God's name isn't written in the book of Esther, His signature flows throughout it in indelible ink. In stroke after stroke of providential script, God masterfully protects His people and preserves the line of promise.

We can't begin to know all the ways God works behind the scenes in our lives, but we can know and trust that He is able to invert even our worst times. He can and does turn our sorrow into joy, our mourning into dancing.

The psalmist writes:

> I will extol thee, O LORD; for thou hast lifted me up, and hast not made my foes to rejoice over me.... For his anger endureth but a moment; in his favour is life: weeping may endure for a night, but joy cometh in the morning.... Thou hast turned for me my mourning into dancing: thou hast put off my sackcloth, and girded me with gladness; to the end that my glory may sing praise to thee, and not be silent. O LORD my God, I will give thanks unto thee for ever (Ps. 30:1, 5, 11–12).

God clothes us with gladness so that we may glorify Him. He puts us into positions of influence within the spheres of our lives for His purpose. At crucial times, we should speak for Him.

Like Esther, may the Spirit equip you to overcome your fears and speak for God. May He turn evil on its head and make you the victor instead of the victim. May you have rest from all your enemies as you rest in Him!

Questions for Reflection

Has God placed me in my current position for a purpose? What might that purpose be?

What specific actions can I take to be bold for God and His people?

How does knowing that God works behind the scenes help me rest in Him today?

9

LONGING EYES

Read: Job 19

*For I know that my redeemer liveth, and that he shall stand
at the latter day upon the earth: and though after my skin
worms destroy this body, yet in my flesh shall I see God:
whom I shall see for myself, and mine eyes shall behold, and
not another.*

—JOB 19:25–27

Throughout the ages Job stands as an example of a righteous
man who suffered. His agony was not a consequence of or
punishment for his sin; he endured trials for reasons that
were completely unknown to him. In the Lord's lengthy
monologue near the end of the book, He didn't tell Job that
his pain proved his love for God or that the account of his
affliction would comfort generations of believers. God gave
no specific reason for Job's suffering; He only proclaimed
His sovereignty.

Each subsequent catastrophe that struck Job intensified,
attacking his possessions, his family, and finally his own
body. Job modeled faith and patience as he received reports
that culminated in the devastating news of his adult children's deaths:

Then Job arose, and rent his mantle, and shaved his
head, and fell down upon the ground, and worshipped,

and said, Naked came I out of my mother's womb, and naked shall I return thither: the LORD gave, and the LORD hath taken away; blessed be the name of the LORD. In all this Job sinned not, nor charged God foolishly (1:20–22).

Job's first response to these deaths was to humble himself in grief and worship. He understood that we own nothing when we come into the world, and we will take nothing from it. We are only temporary stewards. Even when Job's wife urged him to "curse God, and die" (2:9), he did not sin: "But he said unto her, Thou speakest as one of the foolish women speaketh. What? shall we receive good at the hand of God, and shall we not receive evil? In all this did not Job sin with his lips" (2:10).

Despite Job's initial acceptance, the weight of his grief eventually caused him to despair, cursing the day of his birth in chapter 3. This is followed by three exchanges between Job and his friends, who began well by sitting beside him in silence, but later criticized him. They accused him of secret sin that caused these calamities.

God never condemns Job for succumbing to despair. In fact, at the end of the book, He commends Job and condemns the friends (42:7–8). Job's friends have not spoken truthfully about God, but Job has accurately represented Him. God calls Job His servant. Discouragement is not a sin as long as we continue to trust God.

Job 19 relates part of the second round of Job's exchanges with his friends. He expressed his frustration and feelings of isolation. His body wasted away. Yet he marvelously professed faith in a Redeemer he had not yet seen:

> For I know that my Redeemer lives,
>> and at the last he will stand upon the earth.
> And after my skin has been thus destroyed,
>> yet in my flesh I shall see God,
> whom I shall see for myself,
>> and my eyes shall behold, and not another.
>> My heart faints within me! (19:25–27 ESV).

In language that reflects the present, Job confessed a Redeemer who *lives*. He expressed belief not only in the coming Redeemer but also in a bodily resurrection. Thousands of years before Christ's first advent as a helpless baby lying in a manger, Job envisioned Christ's second advent as the powerful God-man standing on the earth.

Job knew his own body would be decayed by then, but he expressed his confidence that it would be resurrected and renewed. Job's eternal soul having reunited with his glorified body, he would see his Redeemer. Job's blood would flow through a pulsating heart. His breath would be inhaled and exhaled through filled lungs. His pupils would dilate at Christ's brightness as Job gazed upon Him with his own longing eyes. Job's whole being yearned to see Christ. He himself would behold his living Redeemer. He would not live that great moment vicariously through another person. No wonder his heart fainted!

Job's longing assures us of our certain future, when our souls will reunite with our resurrected bodies and we will see Christ. This glorious truth comforts us in the loss of loved ones, in life's chronic pain, and in our struggle with sin and its far-reaching effects.

Although Job didn't misrepresent God, he wasn't sinless. God doesn't condemn Job's despair, but He does call him to task for his defiance: "Shall he that contendeth with the Almighty instruct him? he that reproveth God, let him answer it" (40:2).

Job wilts under God's steady stream of questions that demonstrate Job's sinful weakness in comparison to God's holy sovereignty. Bowing in humility, Job repents:

> Who is he that hideth counsel without knowledge? therefore have I uttered that I understood not; things too wonderful for me, which I knew not…. I have heard of thee by the hearing of the ear: but now mine eye seeth thee. Wherefore I abhor myself, and repent in dust and ashes (42:3, 5–6).

Note Job's remarks about now seeing God. He didn't physically see Him as he will at Christ's return, but he had glimpsed God's sovereignty. When adversity flourishes in our lives, who are we, as finite humans, to question the infinite God?

We do well to bear this in mind when we want to scream "why." We don't need to know the reason. We need only to remain faithful. These are better questions: "How can I serve God through this? How does He want me to use this for His glory?"

Accepting God's sovereignty over even our bitter providences calms us in the tempest. Trusting God, even when we don't see a reason for suffering, helps us rest daily in His care and look forward to Christ's return with longing eyes.

Questions for Reflection

What kind of questions am I asking God? Do they reflect acceptance and trust?

How does the hope of seeing my Redeemer comfort me and give me rest in today's struggles?

How can I remind myself of God's sovereignty over everything that happens to me today?

10

BE STILL

Read: Psalms 4 and 27

Stand in awe, and sin not: commune with your own heart upon your bed, and be still.
—PSALM 4:4

Wait on the LORD: be of good courage, and he shall strengthen thine heart: wait, I say, on the LORD.
—PSALM 27:14

The literary fingers of the Psalms feel the pulse of the human heart. No other book of the Bible reflects as wide a range of human emotions. With the psalmists, we climb to heights of joy and plunge to depths of despair. From the loftiest apex to the lowest nadir, and at every point between on the emotional scale, these songs assure us of God's love. They generate within our hearts hope for the uncertain future and peace in the oppressive present. God speaks to our human condition, and we rest in His divine presence.

The psalms swell with so much lovely language promising peace to believers that it's difficult to choose only a few. Although Psalm 23 and others wonderfully comfort believers, we'll explore the concept of rest in some less familiar psalms. Since these brief meditations function like stones skipping across a placid lake, I encourage you to discover much more by diving into the profound depths of all the psalms.

God's desire for us to rest in Him is evident through-out the psalms. Psalm 16:9 proclaims, "Therefore my heart is glad, and my glory rejoiceth: my flesh also shall rest in hope." In Psalm 46, which so beautifully sustains us during global upheaval or personal turmoil, God says, "Be still, and know that I am God" (Ps. 46:10).

The imperative to "be still" also appears in Psalm 4, which begins like many others with a plea for deliverance from enemies. It confesses assurance that God hears the cry of the righteous. Verses 4 and 5 then describe ways to rest in the Lord: "Stand in awe, and sin not: commune with your own heart upon your bed, and be still. Selah. Offer the sac-rifices of righteousness, and put your trust in the LORD."

We are called to reverence God and resist sin. Resisting temptation is more than simply avoiding obvious sins like murder, adultery, and theft. It includes honest assessment of the sins in our hearts: hate, lust, and greed. Although there are differences in degrees of sin and consequences for it, sin is sin. Gossiping about a person in your church is sin, as is shooting someone in the head. Wishing you were married to another man is sin, as is seducing your friend's husband. Scheming for more than your fair share of the family estate is sin, as is robbing your local bank. In quiet and solitary times, we must look deeply into our own hearts to recog-nize and repent from sin. But repentance is more than mere meditation. It involves action.

We must vigorously turn from our sins. Verse 5 tells us to "offer the sacrifices of righteousness." Our offerings of service ought to be motivated by a heart that is not self-righ-teous but rather rests in Christ's righteousness. We must not trust in our own vainglorious and self-centered works but only in Christ's humble and self-sacrificing work.

When we revere Almighty God, repent from our sins, act in real righteousness, and trust in Jesus Christ, we can *be still*. We can securely rest: "I will both lay me down in peace, and sleep: for thou, LORD, only makest me dwell in safety" (4:8).

God alone is the source of our safety and security. The true believer sleeps in peace, resting body and mind in the Lord. This doesn't mean that real Christians will never have a sleepless night or never have to take sleep aids. It does mean, however, that global catastrophes or personal trauma will not completely paralyze us. We continue to function by putting our total trust in God.

Psalm 27 continues the theme of rest while revealing a recurring pattern in the psalms: God promises judgment for the wicked and blessing for the righteous. The more we read the psalms, the more we become convinced that God's promises are not only for the future but also for the present. These are not vague "pie in the sky, try to get by until you die" pledges. Without a doubt, Christ will return to judge the ungodly and condemn them to eternal punishment. But the language in the psalms consistently conveys the *present* character of God's promises. We will not always see the earthly downfall of evil men, but there may be times when we do. We rest in God by trusting His promises for the future and the present.

Psalm 27:1 rhetorically confesses, "The LORD is my light and my salvation; whom shall I fear? the LORD is the strength of my life; of whom shall I be afraid?"

God's Word lights our way; Christ's sacrifice saves our souls. We have all we need for this life and the next. Why should we fear temporary adversity or evil men? The psalmist speaks of his enemies as already fallen: "When the wicked, even mine enemies and my foes, came upon me to eat up my flesh, they stumbled and fell" (27:2). These weren't idle gossips spreading half-truths; these malicious men intended complete destruction. But God brought them down.

The language of Psalm 27 stresses the present: "And *now* shall mine head be lifted up above mine enemies round about me..." (v. 6, emphasis added). "I had fainted, unless I had believed to see the goodness of the LORD *in the land of the living*" (v. 13, emphasis added). The sufferer's head is lifted *now*—while he or she is living on earth.

Psalm 37 reiterates that believers rest now and in the future. Like Psalm 27, it couples that promise with assurances that believers will see the wicked fall:

> Rest in the LORD, and wait patiently for him: fret not thyself because of him who prospereth in his way, because of the man who bringeth wicked devices to pass.... Wait on the LORD, and keep his way, and he shall exalt thee to inherit the land: when the wicked are cut off, thou shalt see it (vv. 7, 34).

Note it's not *if* the wicked are cut off, but *when* they are. And it's something we will surely see. Because we know the destiny of evildoers, we can wait on God's perfect timing with trusting hearts that surge with courage.

Psalm 27's final verse echoes texts we've examined in Deuteronomy, Joshua, and 1 Chronicles: "Wait on the LORD: be of good courage, and he shall strengthen thine heart: wait, I say, on the LORD" (v. 14). Psalm 31:24 repeats the command to be of good courage: "Be of good courage, and he shall strengthen your heart, all ye that hope in the

LORD." By God's gracious Spirit, we wait on His perfect timing with courage and hope.

Questions for Reflection

How does God speak most eloquently to me in these psalms?

What specific steps can I take today that will enable me to *be still*?

How can my actions today reflect a heart filled with hope and courage that rests in God?

11

DWELLING PLACE

Read: Psalm 90

Lord, thou hast been our dwelling place in all generations....
O satisfy us early with thy mercy; that we may rejoice and be
glad all our days.
—PSALM 90:1, 14

Do you have a favorite Bible text? I love too many to narrow my favorite to one passage, and different texts speak more eloquently during different circumstances. But if forced to pick my favorite psalm, I most likely would cite Psalm 90.

This prayer of Moses may seem a rather strange and even morbid choice, since it describes life as futile and fleeting. But I increasingly appreciate the honest realism of this view, particularly couched within the framework of God as our dwelling place.

Consider that Moses never had a real home. As a baby, he was removed from his parental home. He was trained as a youth in the Egyptian palace. As a mature adult, he fled for his life after committing murder and left behind all that power and opulence. This former prince lived in the desert where he worked for his father-in-law as a lowly shepherd. Moses named his son Gershom, meaning "stranger," because, he said, "I have been a stranger in a strange land" (Ex. 2:22). As an old man, Moses led the

Israelites out of Egypt at God's command and remained their leader during forty years of wilderness wanderings. Due to one public sin, he was not permitted to enter the Promised Land, although God allowed him to view it from a mountaintop before taking him to his final resting place and only home.

Moses recognized life's transient character, but he also knew that every believer who ever has lived and who ever will live dwells—not in palaces or tents—but in God. Before God created the earth with its rugged mountain peaks and its surging seas, he chose each believer from the generations of humanity to dwell in Him (vv. 1–2).

God determined the date of your birth, and He has already determined the date of your death (vv. 3, 5). Dates enable our finite minds to mark the passage of time. But God, who is outside the time-and-space continuum, does not measure time as we do. To us, a thousand years is a very long time. Leif Ericsson landed on the North American coast around the year 1000. Papal excommunications finalized the church's split into eastern and western branches in 1054. William the Conqueror led the Norman conquest of England in 1066. These events of the eleventh century are far removed from our twenty-first-century consciousness. But to God, all that intervening time seems as brief as yesterday or a few night hours (v. 4). God is eternal; man is temporal. Man is like grass that springs up in the morning sun but falls beneath the afternoon scythe (vv. 5–6).

Continuing to explore life's transience, Psalm 90 shows that our brief lives are full of trouble, particularly our struggle against sin. God is a holy God who cannot abide sin. The light of His face exposes every secret sin we harbor in our hearts (vv. 7–8). He does this in order to convict us of personal sin. Recognition leads to repentance.

Each sin-filled life is nothing more than a story that has come to "The End" (v. 9). We expend our physical energy on work and our emotional energy on grief. We not only grieve our own sin, but we also grieve the extent of sin's effects. Even if we reach the ripe ages of seventy or eighty, we soon die and our souls fly away (v. 10). Then we will face the holy God who hates sin (v. 11).

Living wisely begins with an awareness of our mortality and sinfulness in contrast to God's infinity and holiness. Moses understood the need to fully utilize each day. In this psalm, he begs God: "So teach us to number our days, that we may apply our hearts unto wisdom. Return, O LORD, how long? and let it repent thee concerning thy servants" (vv. 12–13). Moses knew that an accurate assessment of our finite lives generates biblical wisdom. He knew that we are nothing without God's mercy.

After Moses begs for God's wisdom and pity, he beautifully juxtaposes the contrasts of reality: "O satisfy us early with thy mercy; that we may rejoice and be glad all our days. Make us glad according to the days wherein thou hast afflicted us, and the years wherein we have seen evil" (vv. 14–15).

It is easy to dwell on verse 15's words about afflicted days and evil years, but it is important not to separate it from verse 14. God is able to make us glad, even for the afflicted days and evil years, because His Spirit enables us to rejoice and be glad all our days. Verse 14 in the *English Standard Version* says, "Satisfy us in the morning with your steadfast love, that we may rejoice and be glad all our days." This language recalls Lamentations 3:22–23: "It is of the LORD's mercies that we are not consumed, because his compassions fail not. They are new every morning: great is thy faithfulness." God's mercies never end; He renews them each dawn. His faithfulness is great indeed!

Our faithful God, who every morning renews us with His mercies and satisfies us with His steadfast love, will manifest His work and power in our lives and in the lives of our children (v. 16). God's favor will rest upon believers. And, in spite of our sin and weakness, in spite of our frailty and life's fleetingness, He will establish our efforts: "And let the beauty of the LORD our God be upon us: and establish thou the work of our hands upon us; yea, the work of our hands establish thou it" (v. 17).

Our home is not a rambling ranch or a cozy cottage; our home is not even a faithful family or a saintly spouse. Our home is God. Through all of life's sin and suffering, we can remember that this fallen world is not our home. God is!

With Psalm 90's realistic perspective, we can number our days and become wise. We can be glad all our afflicted days and all our evil years because God will satisfy us each morning with His steadfast love. We can witness His wonders and our children will see His glorious power. And the work we do will not disappear into insignificance. God will rest His favor upon us and establish the work of our hands by giving it meaning.

God is our dwelling place. Welcome home!

Questions for Reflection

In what area of my life do I need to apply my heart unto wisdom?

How does awareness of my sin and finite life help me appreciate God's holiness and infinity?

What does it mean for me today that I rest in God as my dwelling place?

LIFTED EYES

12

Read: Psalm 121

The LORD shall preserve thee from all evil: he shall preserve thy soul. The LORD shall preserve thy going out and thy coming in from this time forth, and even for evermore.

—PSALM 121:7–8

Because these words of Psalm 121 have been set to beautiful music, this psalm sings in my mind more than many others. Aesthetic tunes reflect the glory of the words, which are God's own. When we sing or pray God's words back to Him, we please God. We also hide His words in our hearts. This short psalm overflows with comfort. Singing or reading it fills us with God's peace.

The psalm begins with this well-known and beloved declaration: "I will lift up mine eyes unto the hills, from whence cometh my help. My help cometh from the LORD, which made heaven and earth" (vv. 1–2). As a flatlander of the Midwest, I am always filled with awe for God and His amazing creation when I see majestic mountains. The word "awesome," overused these days almost to the point of triviality, appropriately describes mountains. Who cannot feel God's majesty pierce the heart while seeing a soaring peak pierce the cerulean sky? The upward slope lifts eyes and thoughts from the mundane and temporal to the divine and eternal.

Psalm 121 is the second in fifteen sequential psalms called "songs of ascents." It is believed that pilgrims sang these fifteen psalms on their way to Jerusalem to worship God in the temple. This psalm remains a favorite of travelers today.

As Jewish believers neared Jerusalem, they lifted their eyes to gaze at the hills surrounding the city. Though they had come through many dangers, God had kept them safe and they now approached the security of Jerusalem. Surely the beauty and majesty of the circling peaks filled believers with awe for the God who created them. Similarly, Canadians swivel their heads in awe-filled amazement at the magnificence surrounding them when they drive to Jasper in Alberta. And Americans stop near Jackson in Wyoming to snap pictures of the impressive Tetons rising sharply from the plains.

Artists from the Hudson River School painted sweeping scenes that incredibly conveyed God's grandeur. Their masterpieces often portrayed men or animals as tiny creatures in an expansive landscape dominated by light. Many of these artists intended to create within the viewer a sense of the vast expanse of creation compared to mere man, an infinitesimally small creature in the cosmos, while filling hearts with awe for a wonderful world ruled by *the* Light.

God, the maker of heaven and earth with its majestic mountains, made every person and cares for each believer as a dearly loved individual. Psalm 121 tells us that our heavenly Father watches over us better than any earthly father ever could. Verses 3 and 4 are among the most comforting in Scripture: "He will not suffer thy foot to be moved: he that keepeth thee will not slumber. Behold, he that keepeth Israel shall neither slumber nor sleep."

God will not allow your foot to slip on any slimy surface. God never takes a vacation or a coffee break. He never dozes off, even during our boring prayers or our continual complaints. God keeps each of us with constant and vigilant care.

Psalm 121 continues with a wonderful image of God as a protective covering: "The LORD is thy keeper: the LORD is thy shade upon thy right hand. The sun shall not smite thee by day, nor the moon by night" (vv. 5–6). Think about what it means to be a keeper. As God's image bearers, we are called to care for others and provide for their welfare. After killing his brother, Cain mocked God by asking if he was his brother's keeper (Gen. 4:9). God is not mocked; He saw the evil in Cain's heart and heard Abel's blood cry out from the ground. Cain not only failed to keep his brother, he also failed to keep God's commands. As the original Keeper, God never fails to preserve us.

God protects as a shade on the right hand, the position of authority. He provides powerful protection against the sun's burning rays and the moon's ghostly light. God Himself shades and cools us during blistering days when intense trouble saps our energy as we travel through this arid desert. During lonely nights filled with torments and terrors, God cradles us in the hollow of His hand and comforts us.

Psalm 121's final verses, quoted at the beginning of this meditation, assure us of God's encompassing and eternal care. He keeps your body alive now and your soul alive forever. He protects you from pulsating evil in city streets, from creeping evil in wild creatures, and from menacing evil in human hearts, including your own. Most of all, God protects your eternal soul from everlasting damnation.

As we come and go throughout all of life, God watches over you and me. He was in the delivery room when your eyes blinked open and you broke into your first faltering cries. He will be with you in the nursing home when your eyelids flutter shut and you take your final ragged breath.

God preserves us when we flip down the visor against the sun's morning rays while driving to work and when we return home and unlock the door in the dark. He abides with us through every experience of life, every sting of death, and every joy in heaven. Even beyond that, He will be with us when Christ returns and makes all things new, including these decrepit tents we call our bodies.

Along with Psalm 121, Isaiah 51:6 tells us to lift our eyes: "Lift up your eyes to the heavens, and look upon the earth beneath: for the heavens shall vanish away like smoke, and the earth shall wax old like a garment, and they that dwell therein shall die in like manner: but my salvation shall be for ever, and my righteousness shall not be abolished."

The sky with its vast array of planets and stars will vanish like smoke blown away in the breeze. The solid earth will wear out like an old cloak. All the earth-dwellers whose minds focus only on things below will perish like worn-out rags whose threads deteriorate into nothing. But heaven-dwellers, whose minds are set on things above (Col. 3:2), will be reunited to strong and sturdy bodies. We will be changed. Death will be swallowed up in victory (1 Cor. 15:52–54). We are tiny creatures in a vast cosmos, but we lift our eyes to look at the Light.

Questions for Reflection

What things fill my heart with awe for God?

What fears does Psalm 121 remove from my mind, allowing me to rest in God?

What hope does Psalm 121 give me for the future?

13

QUIET SOUL

Read: Psalms 130 and 131

I wait for the LORD, my soul doth wait,
and in his word do I hope.
—PSALM 130:5

Surely I have behaved and quieted myself.
—PSALM 131:2a

In Psalm 130, we weep with the psalmist's heartrending cry, and like David in Psalm 131, we long to rest in the Lord and quiet our souls. Psalm 130 begins with a plea from the depths of despair: "Out of the depths have I cried unto thee, O LORD. Lord, hear my voice: let thine ears be attentive to the voice of my supplications" (vv. 1–2).

The writer of Psalm 130 bows under the weight of his own sin: "If thou, LORD, shouldest mark iniquities, O Lord, who shall stand? But there is forgiveness with thee, that thou mayest be feared" (vv. 3–4). Perhaps you, like the psalmist, are overcome by the magnitude of personal sin. You wonder how God can possibly forgive all your past offenses and present failings. Do what the psalmist does: turn to the only source of forgiveness, Christ. If God counted our sins against us, we would be bereft of hope. No blemished sinner can stand before God's untainted holiness. But in His great mercy, God forgives!

Because God forgives, believers have hope in His Word: "I wait for the LORD, my soul doth wait, and in his word do I hope. My soul waiteth for the Lord more than they that watch for the morning: I say, more than they that watch for the morning" (vv. 5–6). God's Word fills us with hope and enables us to wait on His will. Standing guard over the city walls in the chill of the deep night before dawn, the watchman longs to see the eastern sky lighten and feel the sun's warming rays. The sufferer from insomnia or chronic pain longs for morning, when a spouse will wake or a friend will call. Nothing seems longer than the solitary watches of the night.

Waiting on God's perfect timing to remedy a situation or reveal His will may be the most difficult lesson to learn in life. We tend to run ahead of God's will. We want things to be fixed, and we want them fixed now. Waiting goes against our nature. But God calls us to meditate in hope and wait with patience.

During our dark nights, we scan the horizon for the piercing pinpoint of the bright and morning star. That star is Christ, who provides merciful and abundant redemption: "Let Israel hope in the LORD: for with the LORD there is mercy, and with him is plenteous redemption. And he shall redeem Israel from all his iniquities" (vv. 7–8).

Although the psalmist longs for deliverance and struggles to wait patiently, he hopes in God. He encourages other believers to hope in the only source of salvation, our merciful Lord. Crying to God and reminding himself of the Lord's complete redemption have lifted him from despair to hope. Christ redeems believers from *all* their iniquities.

The concept of waiting on the Lord logically leads into the quiet soul of Psalm 131. When we learn to wait on the Lord, we recognize our own limitations. We are not able to do everything. We cannot understand all things. But we can learn more and more to lean on the Lord and depend upon His Spirit.

In Psalm 131, David displays total dependence. He begins with honest humility: "Lord, my heart is not haughty, nor mine eyes lofty: neither do I exercise myself in great matters, or in things too high for me" (v. 1). Here is a man who recognizes his limitations. Emulating Christ, he exhibits qualities of a servant leader. His heart is not proud. His demeanor isn't arrogant. David knows that his comprehension is limited and his understanding finite.

Realizing his limits leads David to calm his actions and quiet his soul. This may not have been easy for him. Could anyone be more a man of action than David? He slew the giant. He danced before the ark. He numbered the people. He wanted to build the temple. In 1 Samuel 25 he jumped to judge Nabal and would have killed every male of that household had not Abigail stayed his hand with her good counsel. Ten days later, God struck Nabal dead. David had only to wait on God. He had difficulty learning total dependence, often leaping into action instead of leaning on the Lord.

But when David humbly realized his limits, he was able to depend on God. In Psalm 131, he depicted that total dependence in the vivid imagery of a weaned child: "Surely I have behaved and quieted myself, as a child that is weaned of his mother: my soul is even as a weaned child" (v. 2). A breastfed child can be demanding, nosing and pawing at his mother as he searches for milk. Weaning can be even more stressful. But after the process is complete, the child leans against his mother, calm and content. Once David learned to depend on the Lord, he was at peace. He quieted his soul.

We continue to learn dependence all our lives. It is easier some days, or even some hours, than others. But the more we learn to rest in God, the more our souls quiet.

The lesson of total dependence, however, applies to more than individuals. David expands the concept from himself to the entire body of believers: "Let Israel hope in the LORD from henceforth and for ever" (v. 3). He concludes this short psalm by calling the entire church to hope in the Lord forever.

Are you distressed about a situation in your church? What waves of despair crash over you? Do illness and pain overwhelm you? Do depression and anxiety engulf you? In whatever depth you sink, cry to the Lord. He hears the voice of your supplications.

When you despair, call on God. He is the only source of hope and redemption. Even though you long for His will to be revealed more than watchmen wait for morning, be patient. The morning star will pierce the night. Day will dawn! Lean on the Lord!

Questions for Reflection

In what depths do I find myself today?

How can I wait on the Lord in total dependence?

What steps can I take today to quiet my soul and rest in the Lord?

14

REVIVED SPIRIT

Read: Psalm 143

Cause me to hear thy lovingkindness in the morning; for in thee do I trust: cause me to know the way wherein I should walk; for I lift up my soul unto thee.
—PSALM 143:8

As Christians, we battle the devil, the world, and our own flesh. The war frequently rages on all three fronts. Lustful thoughts lure. Pervasive materialism entices. Numbing depression paralyzes. Exhausted by the continual battle, believers long for final victory. At the very least, they hope for furlough from the front lines. A war-weary David begins Psalm 143 by praying to our faithful and righteous Lord: "Hear my prayer, O LORD, give ear to my supplications: in thy faithfulness answer me, and in thy righteousness. And enter not into judgment with thy servant: for in thy sight shall no man living be justified" (vv. 1–2).

An awareness of personal sin leads David to humbly beg God not to judge him as he deserves. We are all sinners, and we all deserve an eternity in hell. Apart from the atoning work of Christ, no person can be justified.

For David, the battle first flares intensely on the world front: "For the enemy hath persecuted my soul; he hath smitten my life down to the ground; he hath made me to

dwell in darkness, as those that have been long dead. Therefore is my spirit overwhelmed within me; my heart within
me is desolate" (vv. 3–4).

Persecution by enemies (the world) is instigated by evil
forces (the devil) and initiates such intense mental and emotional anguish that David senses his life draining away (the
flesh). He doesn't feel merely like the walking wounded; he
feels like a decaying corpse.

Even though this trial overwhelms his spirit and deso-
lates his heart, David recalls God's goodness: "I remember
the days of old; I meditate on all thy works; I muse on the
work of thy hands. I stretch forth my hands unto thee: my
soul thirsteth after thee, as a thirsty land. Selah" (vv. 5–6).

Recalling God's past gifts of strength and victory leads
David to see His continuing glories in creation. This reflection generates within David a tangible longing, which he
expresses in concrete images. His hands stretch toward
God; his soul thirsts for God like parched earth craves rain.

As David begs God for immediate deliverance, he admits
that he cannot survive without God's mercy:

> Hear me speedily, O LORD: my spirit faileth: hide not
> thy face from me, lest I be like unto them that go down
> into the pit. Cause me to hear thy lovingkindness in the
> morning; for in thee do I trust: cause me to know the
> way wherein I should walk; for I lift up my soul unto
> thee (vv. 7–8).

Like Psalm 90:14 and Lamentations 3:23, verse 8 speaks
of God's mercies in the morning. David asks God to help
him hear His loving promises as each day dawns. This is a
convincing case for thoughtful meditation in early morning
personal devotions.

David confesses his trust in God's steadfast love. But with that trust, he seeks an obedient walk. We've seen trust tied to obedience in previous reflections. The older I get, the more I see the profundity of the title of a hymn I learned as a child, "Trust and Obey." I increasingly realize the need for total dependence upon God—the trust part—and I learn more about submitting my contrary will to His—the obey part.

Trusting and obeying enables us to lift our souls to God and rest in Him. As Psalm 143 progresses, David continues to link obedience with trust: "Deliver me, O LORD, from mine enemies: I flee unto thee to hide me. Teach me to do thy will; for thou art my God: thy spirit is good; lead me into the land of uprightness" (vv. 9–10).

God alone delivers from enemies. In total trust, David flees to Him for refuge. In complete obedience, he requests God's good instruction. He wants God to teach him His will and lead him in righteous living. David's desire to trust and obey is not self-centered: "Quicken me, O LORD, for thy name's sake: for thy righteousness' sake bring my soul out of trouble. And of thy mercy cut off mine enemies, and destroy all them that afflict my soul: for I am thy servant" (vv. 11–12). Certainly David seeks personal relief, but he desires a revived spirit primarily so that God will be glorified. David's deliverance witnesses to God's righteousness.

Note the language of verse 12: David asks God to cut off his enemies out of His mercy. God's justice expresses His love. In His steadfast love, He cuts off believers' enemies: the devil, the world, and the flesh. In His mercy, God destroys every adversary of His servants' souls. Deliverance is reserved for God's servants. It is not for those who talk the talk but fail to walk the walk. Only those who love God and serve Him can expect Him to deliver them from their enemies. God will quench the thirsting souls and revive the failing spirits of those who both trust and obey.

It's difficult to trust God when a wayward child rejects the faith or an abuser traumatizes someone we love. Yet when we trust Him and put our hand in His, we grow into a more intimate relationship with our heavenly Father. He walks beside us, carrying us when necessary, and revives our spirits.

Questions for Reflection

What enemies can I identify on each of the three battle fronts?

How can I trust God and rest in Him in these areas?

In what specific ways can I obey God on the front lines today?

TRUSTING HEART

15

Read: Proverbs 3

Trust in the LORD with all thine heart; and lean not unto thine own understanding. In all thy ways acknowledge him, and he shall direct thy paths.... [Wisdom's] ways are ways of pleasantness, and all her paths are peace.

—PROVERBS 3:5–6, 17

Each meaty verse in Proverbs should be chewed slowly and allowed to digest. As part of the Bible's genre of wisdom literature, Proverbs frequently urges the reader to embrace wisdom. Worldly wisdom resides in postgraduate degrees and status, but biblical wisdom rests in childlike trust and humility.

Proverbs 3 begins by reminding us that peace is possible through knowing and keeping God's law. It then provides the sage advice of verses 5–6.

When I was in fourth grade, autograph books were popular. Friends wrote clever or comical rhymes on the blank pages of the small albums. My mother finally purchased an autograph book for me. As I leafed through its crisp white pages, I eagerly anticipated asking friends to write their favorite of the circulating verses. After several friends had written various hilarious witticisms, I decided to do something no one else had done: I would ask my teacher to write in my autograph book.

She solemnly accepted the book and promised to return it after the noon recess. When I came back to her desk, she handed it to me with a face that seemed even more serious than usual. During class, I surreptitiously snuck a glance to see what she'd written. In perfect penmanship, she had inscribed the words of Proverbs 3:5–6. I quickly shut the book and put it away, my face flushed. I confess that my fourth-grade mind thought writing a Bible verse in an autograph book was a little strange. I felt twinges of anger as well as embarrassment.

Know what? I can't remember a single one of my friends' witty scribbles or even which friends wrote in my book. But I remember my teacher's grave face when she gave the book back to me. And I've never forgotten what she wrote. From fourth grade throughout my entire life, God has continued to teach me how to trust Him rather than leaning on my own understanding.

That trust shouldn't be apathetic, but wholeheartedly dependent. Perhaps the concept of dependence conveys negative connotations. It may even bring to mind helpless disabled people or a person in a relationship who is controlled or manipulated by another. Ours is a culture of hardy independence. We value self-reliance. Giving up control goes against our natural inclinations. We believe we know best. But if we're truly wise, we will depend upon God, not on our physical or mental abilities.

Verse 6 indicates that when we acknowledge God as Lord over every area of life, He will direct our paths. Direction implies both guidance and sovereignty. God guides us in particular paths He has ordained and is controlling for our good and His glory. These *ways* and *paths* express action. Mentally acknowledging Christ's lordship isn't enough; we must physically demonstrate His lordship by walking in His ways.

Proverbs 3:7 repeats the command to reject self-centered wisdom in favor of revering and obeying God. Subsequent verses delineate material blessings for those who honor God by living according to His principles. But they don't promise all blessings all the time. This is no health-and-wealth gospel. Verses 11–12 confirm that we will suffer, but even this is from the Lord. The next several verses extol biblical wisdom, elevating its value above expensive silver, fine gold, and precious rubies.

Our final focus verse is sandwiched between two that personify wisdom as a woman granting long and prosperous life and as a tree of life bearing the fruit of happiness. Proverbs 3:17 centers our attention on rest: "Her ways are ways of pleasantness, and all her paths are peace." Again we see the emphasis on physical activity as well as mental assent. Walking in wisdom produces pleasant ways and peaceful paths. We daily rest in the Lord by wholeheartedly trusting Him and doing His will. That is the path of biblical wisdom.

Verses 23–26 of Proverbs 3 describe wisdom as God's instrument for creating and maintaining the cosmos before again urging the reader to acquire wisdom's precepts. Sound wisdom and discretion are life to the soul and grace to the body. They enable you to rest in the Lord by day and night:

> Then shalt thou walk in thy way safely, and thy foot shall not stumble. When thou liest down, thou shalt not be afraid: yea, thou shalt lie down, and thy sleep shall be sweet. Be not afraid of sudden fear, neither of

> the desolation of the wicked, when it cometh. For the
> LORD shall be thy confidence, and shall keep thy foot
> from being taken.

Confidence in God permits you to walk safely and to sleep sweetly. You need not fear sudden calamity or final Armageddon. Whatever happens to you today or far into the future, God will preserve even your lowly foot. He numbers every hair on your head (Matt. 10:30); not one of them falls without His knowledge and permission.

Proverbs 3 continues with several verses guiding godly behavior: do good to others when you are able, do not scheme evil against your neighbor, don't contend with those who haven't harmed you, don't envy oppressors and choose their ways (vv. 27–31).

Why choose the way of the oppressor when you can choose the way of the Lord?

The concluding verses of Proverbs 3 juxtapose the wicked with the righteous. The devious are an abomination to God, but He takes the righteous into His confidence. He curses the house of the wicked, but blesses the habitation of the just. He scorns scorners, but gives grace to the humble. He confers shame to fools, but bequeaths glory to the wise.

Don't depend on your own intelligence. Walk in the pleasant ways and peaceful paths of biblical wisdom. Trust in the Lord with all your heart!

Questions for Reflection

Which morsels from Proverbs 3 speak most directly to me today—and why?

In what ways do I lean on myself, and how can I lean more on God as I go about my tasks today?

In what specific ways can I rest in the Lord by seeking the peaceful paths of biblical wisdom today?

16

FEAR NOT

Read: Isaiah 43

But now thus saith the LORD that created thee, O Jacob, and he that formed thee, O Israel, Fear not: for I have redeemed thee, I have called thee by thy name; thou art mine.

—ISAIAH 43:1

The prophet Isaiah declared judgment on the people of Israel who had rejected God, but he also proclaimed stirring prophesies and comforting promises. And he relayed God's frequent command to fear not. That mandate nestles within predictions about Christ and descriptions of God in Isaiah 40: "O Jerusalem, that bringest good tidings, lift up thy voice with strength; lift it up, be not afraid; say unto the cities of Judah, Behold your God!" (v. 9).

In Isaiah's next chapter, the "fear not" imperative crescendos as it appears three times in verses of great comfort:

Fear thou not; for I am with thee: be not dismayed; for I am thy God: I will strengthen thee; yea, I will help thee; yea, I will uphold thee with the right hand of my righteousness…. For I the LORD thy God will hold thy right hand, saying unto thee, Fear not; I will help thee. Fear not, thou worm Jacob, and ye men of Israel; I will

help thee, saith the LORD, and thy redeemer, the Holy
One of Israel (41:10, 13–14).

Some of this language recalls assurances we've read throughout the Old Testament: God declares that He is with us,
He encourages us not to be dismayed, and He promises to
strengthen us. Here God also pledges to uphold us, help us,
and redeem us.

Compared to God's holiness, all people—even God's
chosen ones in the Old Testament and today—are as lowly
as worms. But Christ, the Holy One, redeems believers
and gives us everlasting value. He unites us with the eternal
Godhead and the universal church. He promises to uphold
us with His hand of power, depicting His sustaining grace
like a father holding the hand of a little child.

In Isaiah 43, God confirms His sovereign care for
His people and His personal concern for individuals. He
reminds us that He formed each one of us in our mother's
womb (Ps. 139:13). He reminds us that because He has
redeemed us, we need not fear.

While you grew in the womb, your parents may have
spent many hours discussing names and determining one
they felt was perfect for you. But God has His own name
for you. He declares that He has called you by your name,
and you are His. Being His dear child, however, doesn't
exclude you from suffering. Just as an earthly father sometimes teaches his child painful lessons, our heavenly Father
allows pain in our lives for His good purpose. But He does
not leave us alone. In Isaiah 43:2, God promises to walk
with us in even our most overwhelming trials: "When thou
passest through the waters, I will be with thee; and through
the rivers, they shall not overflow thee: when thou walkest

through the fire, thou shalt not be burned; neither shall the flame kindle upon thee."

Whether our home is destroyed by the flooding Mississippi or a surging Indonesian tsunami, God is with us. When we pass through the river of death, God will be with us. When anxiety overwhelms or depression numbs, He is with us. Just as He walked with Shadrach, Meshach, and Abednego in the fiery furnace, He is with us when we walk in the furnace of affliction. He walks beside you in your trauma, grief, or pain.

The Israelites were destined for the fiery trial of exile, but God promises that He will be with them and restore them. He again assures them of His presence and purpose: "Fear not: for I am with thee…. Even every one that is called by my name: for I have created him for my glory, I have formed him; yea, I have made him" (vv. 5, 7).

God has created each one of us for His glory. When the Father created people, He imbued them with complex emotions. Christ came to earth and lived as a real man with human emotions. Our triune God understands every aspect of our nature, including our propensity to fear. We fear natural disaster, atrocious war, sudden accident, inexorable cancer, helpless indignity, and inevitable death. Bumper stickers proclaiming "No Fear" lie. We may feel unafraid at times, but it is impossible for anyone to be constantly without fear. That is why God must repeatedly tell us, "Fear not."

Christ did, however, tell His followers to fear one thing: "And fear not them which kill the body, but are not able to kill the soul: but rather fear him which is able to destroy both soul and body in hell" (Matt. 10:28). He told them to fear Himself! Jesus Christ is the judge who will condemn unbelievers to an eternity of body and soul destruction in hell. But He is also the Savior who redeems the souls and will glorify the bodies of believers to an eternity of fellowship with God in heaven!

Isaiah portrays our Redeemer as our primary reason not to be afraid:

> I, even I, am the LORD; and beside me there is no saviour. I have declared, and have saved, and I have shewed... therefore ye are my witnesses, saith the LORD, that I am God. Yea, before the day was I am he; and there is none that can deliver out of my hand: I will work, and who shall let it?
>
> Thus saith the LORD, your redeemer, the Holy One of Israel.... I am the LORD, your Holy One, the creator of Israel, your King (vv. 11–15).

Even though God's people were conquered and exiled, God remained their Savior and their God. He existed before He called the first day into being. No one thwarts His plan. He is the Lord, the Holy One, the Creator, and our King.

Since this is our last look at an Old Testament passage, it's interesting to note the connection to creation, which was the subject of our first reflection. God Himself unites His work as Creator with His atonement as Savior and His reign as King. God pledges to do a "new thing" by making "a way in the wilderness, and rivers in the desert" (v. 19). He promises, "I, even I, am he that blotteth out thy transgressions for mine own sake, and will not remember thy sins" (v. 25). God grants a new life-giving way of salvation through Christ, who blots all our sins from divine memory.

When you are afraid, remind yourself of God's command to fear not. Remember that Christ is the only one capable of destroying both body and soul. If you believe in Him, He has redeemed you and you are His. Because He created and named you, He knows you intimately. He understands your fears. He walks with you through every overwhelming flood and each devastating fire. Grasp His hand and walk with Him!

Questions for Reflection

What does it mean to me that God created and named me?

How does my relationship with Christ and resting in Him affect my greatest fear?

In what specific ways can I go forward fearlessly today?

17

LIGHT YOKE

Read: Matthew 11

Come unto me, all ye that labour and are heavy laden, and I will give you rest. Take my yoke upon you, and learn of me; for I am meek and lowly in heart: and ye shall find rest unto your souls. For my yoke is easy, and my burden is light.
—MATTHEW 11:28–30

Are you so overwhelmed with stress and responsibilities that you feel like the proverbial camel straining under a heavy load? Does it seem you can't handle even one more straw? The bad news is that you have to take one more thing upon yourself. The good news is that you will find rest for your soul, which is very good news indeed!

At the end of Matthew 11, Christ addresses workers burdened with heavy loads. Your work may be preaching sermons, or it may be changing diapers. Perhaps you are unable to do any work due to physical limitations. The pastor bows beneath constant sermon preparation and grave congregational concerns. The young mother bends to clinging toddler demands and increasing laundry piles. The disabled person cringes under chronic pain and hopeless inactivity. You know the weight of your own load.

Whatever work or worry weighs us down, Christ tells us to take His yoke upon ourselves. A farmer controls an ox in the field with a yoke. The *u*-shaped wooden device has a bar across the top holding it in place on the ox's neck. The yoke keeps the ox from turning to the right or left; as long as he looks straight ahead, the yoke's weight is evenly distributed. But if the ox resists the yoke and tries to twist out of it, it chafes him. The farmer uses the yoke to keep the ox moving forward, plowing straight furrows.

We take Christ's yoke upon our necks by submitting our wills to His and allowing Him to guide us. His yoke isn't onerous or heavy. When we follow His direction without turning aside, we hardly notice the weight. We plow straight.

Many of us go about our daily work, trying to view it as God's calling, but not really connecting the dots. Our work doesn't seem to achieve any good in God's kingdom. We don't change any lives or do anything of lasting significance. Hours grind away in monotonous repetition. Daily refreshment eludes us.

We rush from one day to the next, longing for the weekend. Our weekends quickly fill with hectic activities, and we feel weary as we begin our work week. We may have attended church on Sunday, but we've missed Sabbath rest. How do the weary find rest? Jesus promises soul rest to those who learn from His meekness and humility.

In submission to God's will, Christ left His glory in heaven and humbled Himself to life and death on earth (Phil. 2:1–11). When we submit our contrary wills to Christ's, we imitate His model of meekness. But meekness doesn't mean drudgery.

Jesus lived in Sabbath awareness, delighting in God's daily goodness. He enjoyed food, drink, and friendships. He embraced life so heartily that the Jewish leaders criticized Him in Matthew 11, leading Him to say about them: "The

Son of man came eating and drinking, and they say, Behold a man gluttonous, and a winebibber, a friend of publicans and sinners. But wisdom is justified of her children" (v. 19). These Jewish leaders were more concerned with trivial external behavior than with crucial internal faith. This evidenced their hard hearts and witnessed to their lack of real wisdom. The truly wise person submits to Christ with a meek and humble attitude. The submissive spirit finds that Christ's yoke is light and life can be enjoyed.

Christ modeled festive Sabbath rest and taught, "The sabbath was made for man, and not man for the sabbath" (Mark 2:27). Sabbath rest is never a matter of legalistic rules; it is a heart attitude. Sabbath rest worships and listens to God's Word. It prays and cares for the needy. It fellowships and feasts.

If we observe Sabbath as a festive day of rest, our heart's attitude will spill into our daily routine. We can find meaning in our work. Wherever we labor and whether or not our work is appreciated, we find rest by imitating Christ's humility. Even if our labor consists only of patience and prayer, our souls rest by submitting to Christ.

Those who resist Christ's yoke demonstrate hardness of heart. The hard hearts of the leaders and some Jewish cities led Christ to pray: "I thank thee, O Father, Lord of heaven and earth, because thou hast hid these things from the wise and prudent, and hast revealed them unto babes. Even so, Father: for so it seemed good in thy sight" (vv. 25–26). Jesus thanked God for revealing Him to the humble believers who had childlike faith, and not to the self-righteous and hypocritical religious leaders. The religious rulers were wise in their own eyes, but their knowledge consisted of burdensome regulations. Their yoke was heavy. Simple believers in Christ understood more about the kingdom of heaven than the learned leaders. Christ ended His prayer with a confirmation that God views His revelation to the humble as good.

Jesus then explained that the Father has given Him all authority, and He is the revelation of God. The Father and Son know each other intimately, but no one can know the Father, except those to whom the Son chooses to reveal Him (v. 27).

If Christ has revealed the Father to you, you will gladly take His yoke upon your neck. You will bend your will to His and follow His example of gentle humility. Don't fight the yoke! Let it rest on your shoulders and move forward with hope!

"He that hath ears to hear, let him hear" (v. 15).

Questions for Reflection

In what ways do I fight Christ's yoke or turn aside from it?

What changes should I make in my Sabbath observance?

In what specific ways today can I submit to Christ's will and rest in Him?

IMPOSSIBLE REALITIES

18

Read: Mark 10

*And Jesus looking upon them saith, With men it is impossible,
but not with God: for with God all things are possible.*

—MARK 10:27

Today's focus text is one of many biblical gems we often
pull from memory's treasury to brighten dark days with
its brilliance. While storing Scripture in our minds is the
best accumulation of wealth, sometimes we take a jewel
out of context and fail to see the beauty of its golden fili-
gree setting. This text comforts us when we face daunting
tasks that challenge the limits of our abilities or when we
attempt kingdom work that appears impossible. But when
we look at the historical context, we see another facet glint
in the light.

Mark 10 begins with the Pharisees trying to trap Jesus
into a compromising answer about divorce, looking for an
excuse to accuse Him. As He frequently did, Jesus responded
with a question of His own to turn their question on its
head. Using language often echoed in wedding ceremonies,
Christ declares marriage as a creation ordinance.

After inverting the Pharisees' teaching on divorce, Jesus
welcomed little children into His arms in one of Scripture's

most touching vignettes. Certainly Jesus loved and still loves little children. But His love for children wasn't His point. Surrounded by these visual aids, He stressed the necessity for childlike faith: "Whosoever shall not receive the kingdom of God as a little child, he shall not enter therein" (v. 15). This is especially convicting since it follows Christ's contradiction of hypocritical teaching and hard hearts. Internal faith is more important than external religion. Pious living means nothing unless it springs from true piety, the simple faith of a soft heart.

After the tender scene of Christ blessing children, Mark relates the story that supplies our text. A young man eagerly ran to Jesus and fell on his knees before Him, asking what he needed to do to inherit eternal life. Knowing the young man's heart differed from his outward enthusiasm, Jesus immediately pricked his pride: "Why callest thou me good? there is none good but one, that is, God" (v. 18).

Jesus clearly conveyed that the young man was not as righteous as he thought. No one is good except God. Christ wasn't implying that He didn't deserve to be called good. Rather, He wanted this fellow to recognize his sin and think about whom he addressed. Was he speaking to a mere man and excellent teacher? No, he faced the only truly good person who ever walked on earth: the man who was God.

Jesus wanted the young man to look into the depths of his heart and examine its motivation. When Christ listed commandments dealing with human relationships, the man's smug answer indicated his proud heart. Then Jesus hit him where it really hurt: his wallet. The man went away sad, but he just couldn't give up his wealth to follow Christ.

Because in the Old Testament God often promised material blessings for those who were godly, the Jewish mentality viewed a prosperous person as particularly righteous. This was another perception Jesus turned upside down. He declared that it was difficult for a rich man to enter the kingdom of heaven, repeating it three times for emphasis. In fact, Jesus said it was easier for a camel to pass through the eye of a needle! Whether He referred to the tiny slot in a sewing needle or to a small opening in an ancient wall, His point was plain: wealth is not an evidence of faith, but generally hampers humble faith. The disciples' surprise forms the immediate context of today's focus verse: "And they were astonished out of measure, saying among themselves, Who then can be saved? And Jesus looking upon them saith, With men it is impossible, but not with God: for with God all things are possible" (vv. 26–27).

After everything the disciples had seen Jesus do (including raising the dead, walking on water, and calming the storm), it seems odd that they reacted to this teaching with such amazement. They had yet to learn that men can do nothing to obtain salvation, but God does it all. With Him, there is no distinction between rich and poor; all believers are one in Christ Jesus (Gal. 3:28). The free gift of salvation is impossible with man, but with God all things—even the salvation of your eternal soul—are possible!

Certainly God can make it possible for you to bear your chronic pain. He absolutely can make it possible for your tiny church plant to succeed. Struggles are proper times to behold the beauty of this gem. But we also see it glint as a brilliant reminder of God's saving grace, expressed so well by John Newton:

> Amazing grace! How sweet the sound
> That saved a wretch like me!
> I once was lost, but now am found;
> Was blind, but now I see.

Christ carries me through impossible days and interminable nights because He first saved a wretch like me, the chief of wicked sinners (1 Tim. 1:15).

Christ concluded this conversation with a final inversion: "But many that are first shall be last; and the last first" (v. 31). The disciples continued to be amazed—and afraid (v. 32). At this point, there was much they didn't understand, particularly about Christ as the Suffering Servant who would give His life as a ransom for His chosen ones.

Mark's account segues into Christ's description of His impending humiliation, followed by James's and John's incredible request for self-glory. Christ utilizes this as a springboard for crucial instruction about servant leadership: "Whosoever will be great among you, shall be your [servant]: and whosoever of you will be the chiefest, shall be servant of all. For even the Son of man came not to be [served], but to [serve], and to give his life as a ransom for many" (vv. 43–45).

Jesus gave His life to redeem many. Are you one of them? If you are, then you will imitate His servant leadership by humbly ministering to others. The Suffering Servant died for poor sinners like you and me. If we love Him with childlike faith, we will see our Father in heaven.

If Christ died to accomplish your unattainable salvation, you can trust Him to do the impossible in your life. Gaze at all this gem's glinting facets in the Light!

Questions for Reflection

In what ways does the context of today's focus verse expand my understanding of it?

What personal religiosity do I need to abandon and instead trust Christ with childlike faith while I rest in Him?

In what specific areas can I trust God to do the impossible in my life today?

19

BANISHED ANXIETY

Read: Luke 12:1–34

Fear not, little flock; for it is your Father's good pleasure to give you the kingdom.

—LUKE 12:32

Few things feel more like spiritual warfare than full-blown anxiety. Its insidious symptoms attack randomly. Palpitations shake the chest and steal its victim's breath. Panic penetrates every pore. Associations trigger it, or it flares for no apparent reason. Relief comes more through learning to trust and cope than looking for a cause or cure.

As with depression, grief, and every other malady known to mankind, believers are not exempt from anxiety. But they can diminish the kind of anxiety that is rooted in worry. And in Luke 12, the physician Luke writes God's prescription. He first records how Christ warned His disciples against the Pharisaical leaven of hypocrisy. Hypocrites pretend to be righteous when their hearts are hard. Like leaven spreads through dough, such deception permeates a congregation. Jesus then cautioned His followers regarding hypocritical deceptions and behind-the-scenes manipulations: "For there is nothing covered, that shall not be revealed; neither hid, that shall not be known. Therefore whatsoever ye have spoken in darkness shall be heard in the light; and that which ye have spoken in the ear in closets shall be proclaimed upon the housetops" (vv. 2–3).

What uncomfortable scenarios! Every midnight remark and each whispered word will be proclaimed from rooftops. Our "secret" or "private" conversations are being recorded, not by hidden bugs or wiretaps, but by an omniscient and omnipresent God.

God is not only aware of every word that falls from our lips, but He is also aware of every hair that falls from our heads: "Are not five sparrows sold for two farthings, and not one of them is forgotten before God? But even the very hairs of your head are all numbered. Fear not therefore: ye are of more value than many sparrows" (vv. 6–7).

God bears in mind the lowliest bird in creation. He knows how many hairs remain on your brush each morning and how many fall to your shoulders during the day. If He knows these trivialities, we can trust He will remember us.

He knows exactly how much adrenaline courses through our veins and every pang of anxiety that causes. He knows how terrifying it is for you to face your bullying boss and possible job loss. But He is with you in all this. Why should we be afraid or anxious?

Perhaps you worry about serious issues you might face in the future—like persecution—and fear that you will deny Christ. After all, Luke 12:9 warns that anyone who denies Christ before men will be denied before the angels. And the next verse warns that anyone who blasphemes the Holy Spirit commits the unforgivable sin.

What is this unforgivable sin? It might help to first look at what it is not. It is not promiscuity, adultery, homosexuality, abortion, suicide, or murder. All these sins can be forgiven.

It is not even denial of Christ: "And whosoever shall speak a word against the Son of man, it shall be forgiven him" (Luke 12:10). The account in John 21:15–19 shows how Christ lovingly forgave Peter after he denied Him.

Matthew and Mark related the unforgivable sin to Christ's miracles (Matt. 12:31–32; Mark 3:28–29). The scribes accused Christ of having demonic power, which revealed their hard hearts and impenitent spirits despite Christ's vivid displays of triune divinity. Although theologians may differ slightly in definitions of the unforgivable sin, it seems clear that it involves blatant rejection of the Spirit—a sin impossible for a repentant believer to commit. A fear of having committed the unforgivable sin indicates the Spirit's work in your heart and assures you that you have *not* committed it.

True Christians need not fear committing a sin that cannot be forgiven. Christ assures believers that they don't have to worry about what they might face in the future: "And when they bring you unto the synagogues, and unto magistrates, and powers, take ye no thought how or what thing ye shall answer, or what ye shall say: for the Holy Ghost shall teach you in the same hour what ye ought to say" (vv. 11–12).

Many people's hearts flutter when they are asked to pray in a group. Most people get nervous about speaking to a large audience. Anyone would worry prior to being grilled and possibly maligned on a witness stand. We can't know what we would say under torture. But Christ promised that the Holy Spirit will give believers the very words they need to speak at such moments. What marvelous comfort!

We don't have to worry about the future or the present. Dr. Luke leads into his antianxiety prescription by relating a request and a parable. A man's estate arbitration request led

Jesus to tell a parable about a man who built bigger barns, but died before he could enjoy his increased possessions. Christ concluded: "So is he that layeth up treasure for himself, and is not rich toward God" (Luke 12:21).

Christ then assures Christians that they need not worry about food or clothing. God cares for the ravens. Will He not also care for you? Worrying adds nothing to life, but only detracts from its enjoyment. Even the royal robes of King Solomon appeared drab compared to a lily's exquisite beauty. If God cares for transient plants, He will surely care for His own children. We should not worry about provisions or be plagued by doubts. God knows our needs. Rather than pursuing possessions, believers should seek the advancement of God's kingdom: "But rather seek ye the kingdom of God; and all these things shall be added unto you. Fear not, little flock; for it is your Father's good pleasure to give you the kingdom" (Luke 12:31–32). Why worry about food or clothing when you have the kingdom of God? The Great Shepherd enjoys bestowing His little flock with His kingdom's staggering bounty.

Anxiety may strike and momentarily paralyze even the godliest saint, but believers can increasingly banish it by worrying less and trusting more. Rest in the Lord, who numbers your very hairs. Don't fear the future, even persecution, because the Spirit will guide your words. God cares for His flock. He loves giving believers the best gifts from His kingdom's abundance. In fact, He gives them the entire kingdom!

Those who love the Lord can rest in God's loving care. Christ said, "For where your treasure is, there will your heart be also" (Luke 12:34). Where's your heart?

Questions for Reflection

How will I change my speech patterns today, knowing that every word I say will be broadcast?

How does knowing that God loves to give me His entire kingdom affect my tendency to worry?

In what specific ways can I rest in God's loving care by evidencing my heart's treasure today?

UNTROUBLED HEART

20

Read: John 14

Let not your heart be troubled: ye believe in God, believe also in me…. Peace I leave with you, my peace I give unto you: not as the world giveth, give I unto you. Let not your heart be troubled, neither let it be afraid.
—JOHN 14:1, 27

The setting: the upper room. The scene: Christ with His disciples. The subject: His touching farewell on the eve of His crucifixion. You can imagine the disciples' solemn faces as they grieve their beloved teacher's imminent departure, their puzzled expressions as they attempt to understand. You can almost hear the gentle tone of Christ's voice in His assurances.

When they read John 14, believers in this cold world feel Christ's words wrap comfort around them like layers of warm blankets. The first and last layers are Christ's touching words: "Let not your heart be troubled."

Our hearts are often troubled in this sorrow-filled world. We worry. We are concerned about jobs, living situations, and loved ones. We grieve on multiple levels. Bodies weaken. Memories lag. Friends desert. Spouses die. Leaders betray. We sin.

But in the solemn setting of that upper room and still today, Christ tells His disciples and all believers not to allow their hearts to be troubled. Why? Because the triune God gives believers peace.

John 14 relates promise after promise of Christ's continuing care for us now and His guaranteed hope for our glorious future. He promises to prepare our place in heaven (v. 2). He promises to return and bring us into fellowship with Him there (v. 3). He promises Himself as the only way of salvation and as truth and life (v. 6). Whatever believers ask in His name, He promises to do for the Father's glory (vv. 13–14). But He primarily promises peace and comfort.

Christ would ask the Father to send another Comforter, the Spirit of truth, to be with His people forever (vv. 16–17). Believers will not be as bereft as orphans (v. 18) because the Spirit will live in them, uniting them to the triune God (vv. 19–20).

God the Holy Spirit is a comforter: "I, even I, am he that comforteth you" (Isa. 51:12). The Spirit comforts us when we are ill, lonely, in pain, or when we grieve. Through the Spirit we are blessed with fellowship, consolation in Christ, and loving comfort (Phil. 2:1). The Spirit comforts us by guaranteeing our eternal destiny. Paul speaks of the Spirit as an "earnest" (2 Cor. 1:22, 5:5), which simply means a down payment. The Spirit is a deposit in our hearts that guarantees our heavenly home. The Comforter witnesses in our hearts to Christ's truth: "But when the Comforter is come, whom I will send unto you from the Father, even the Spirit of truth, which proceedeth from the Father, he shall testify of me" (John 15:26).

Before He left this earth, Christ assured believers of His unity with the Father (v. 11). In what has become known as His High Priestly Prayer, He prayed for our unity with the divine Trinity: "That they all may be one; as thou, Father, art in me, and I in thee, that they also may be one in us… that they may be one, even as we are one: I in them, and thou in me, that they may be made perfect in one" (John 17:21–23). Christ prayed for all true believers to be united with each other and in God. Lowly humans are united to the triune God! Can we begin to comprehend this vast and profound mystery?

Paul writes about this mysterious union in Ephesians: "For we are members of his body, of his flesh, and of his bones. For this cause shall a man leave his father and mother, and shall be joined unto his wife, and they two shall be one flesh. This is a great mystery: but I speak concerning Christ and the church" (Eph. 5:30–32).

Our fellowship with Christ should be as intimate as the relationship between a husband and wife. This is indeed a great mystery, which deserves deep and continual contemplation. The creation of Eve as the perfect helpmeet for Adam may have been less about meeting his needs than about depicting Christ's relationship with His church.

Within that close relationship, Christians show their love by obeying God's Word: "If ye love me, keep my commandments" (v. 15). Christ speaks of this loving obedience in relationship with the triune God:

> He that hath my commandments, and keepeth them, he it is that loveth me: and he that loveth me shall be loved of my Father, and I will love him, and will manifest myself to him…. If a man love me, he will keep my words: and my Father will love him, and we will come unto him, and make our abode with him. He that loveth me not keepeth not my sayings: and the word

which ye hear is not mine, but the Father's which sent
me (vv. 21–24).

Notice that Christ speaks in the plural here: "*We* will
come unto him, and make *our* abode with him." Christ
didn't come to earth on an individual mission. He lived and
worked as part of the Trinity. His teaching came from the
Father. And that same teaching would lodge in believers'
hearts and minds through the comforting presence of the
Holy Spirit: "But the Comforter, which is the Holy Ghost,
whom the Father will send in my name, he shall teach you
all things, and bring all things to your remembrance, whatsoever I have said unto you" (v. 26).

If you believe in Christ for salvation, He did not leave
you alone. He gave you the amazing gift of His peace, which
differs dramatically from the world's. The world looks at
peace as relief from war or oppression with the freedom
for every individual to pursue personal goals. God's peace is
reconciliation with Himself through Christ's redemption.
His peace passes all understanding. It is the Spirit living
in your heart, granting you a calm spirit despite trials and
struggles. The triune God's peace enables your heart not to
be troubled or afraid (v. 27).

You dwell in unity with the divine Trinity. Christ's body
in heaven and His Spirit in your heart guarantee your eternal dwelling in glory. The Spirit daily comforts you in your
struggles and sorrows. Why be afraid? Why allow your heart
to be troubled?

Questions for Reflection

What things trouble my heart, and how can I view them differently so that I can experience rest?

How does my unity with the triune God change the way I live with other believers?

In what ways can I demonstrate the Holy Spirit's comfort to others today?

21

GOOD CHEER

Read: Acts 27

And now I exhort you to be of good cheer: for there shall be no loss of any man's life among you, but of the ship. For there stood by me this night the angel of God, whose I am, and whom I serve, saying, Fear not, Paul; thou must be brought before Caesar: and, lo, God hath given thee all them that sail with thee. Wherefore, sirs, be of good cheer: for I believe God, that it shall be even as it was told me.

—ACTS 27:22–25

Acts 27 relates a suspenseful account of difficult sailing and perilous shipwreck. Contrary winds created dangerous delays. Soft southerly winds turned into a tumultuous northeastern gale. Driven before the wind and tossed by the tempest, the sailors tried everything humanly possible to save the ship and their lives. But after many sunless days and starless nights, they relinquished all hope.

At this bleak moment during a black night, Paul appeared in the midst of the spent and hopeless men to bring this word from the Lord: "Be of good cheer" (v. 22). Paul assured them that, even though the ship would sink, not one of the 276 lives on board would be lost. An angel of God told Paul, "Fear not" (v. 24). As Paul reiterated the imperative to "be of good cheer," he confessed, "for I believe God" (v. 25).

Being of good cheer goes beyond mere cheerfulness. These men were terrified of drowning in the depths of a stormy sea. They needed far more than a simple "Cheer up!" Paul didn't ask them to put a happy face mask over their frightened visages. Good cheer here conveys courage rooted in confident hope. It is more like "Take heart!" or "Keep up your courage!" This cheer uproots terror and fills the heart with peace. The element of courage brings to mind God's command to "be strong and of a good courage" (Deut. 31:6–7; Josh. 1:6).

Tossed about in the creaking hold of a foundering Egyptian grain ship, Paul had peace. He was able to obey the angel's directive to fear not. He could take heart for one simple reason: he believed God.

When we're tossed on life's turbulent seas, an angel doesn't miraculously appear by our side with a direct word from God. Neon lights providing personal direction don't glow in the night sky. But God reveals Himself to us in His Word. Just as surely as the word of God came to Paul through the mouth of the angel, His word pulses between the worn leather covers of your Bible.

Like Paul, we can believe God. We can take Him at His word because His word is truth (John 17:17). It never fails (Isa. 34:16). Everything God decrees shall come to pass. Not one word will ever return to Him void (Isa. 55:11). When He says, "Be of good cheer," we can do it because we can believe Him.

God promised Paul that the lives of all the people in the ship would be saved. This word from the Lord was so sure that the angel presented it in the past tense: "God *hath given* thee all them that sail with thee" (v. 24, emphasis added).

God's rescue was so certain that the angel spoke of it as something already accomplished.

God doesn't promise us freedom from shipwreck or death; however, He does promise the true believer will suffer no loss of everlasting life. When swept by tempests, we can take heart. Our ships of pride, self-righteousness, bitterness, anger, or fear may sink. Breath may cease and heart stop, but the believer's eternal soul will never be lost.

This confirms Scripture's continual teaching not to be afraid. Time after time we've seen God's command to fear not (Gen. 15:1; Ex. 20:20; Deut. 31:8; 2 Kings 6:16; Isa. 43:1; Luke 12:32). Obviously God knows our weak nature and how human emotions fluctuate. He knows how difficult it is for us to face frightening circumstances without fear. But He commands us not to be afraid because He has already determined the outcome. He controls even the most devastating events. We can have faith in God. We can trust that things will be exactly as He tells us in His Word: "I will never leave thee, nor forsake thee. So that we may boldly say, The Lord is my helper, and I will not fear what man shall do unto me" (Heb. 13:5–6). We also have Christ's promise to be with us always. Before He left this earth, He said, "Lo, I am with you always, even unto the end of the world" (Matt. 28:20).

God has promised always to be with us. Do we live as if we really believe this? When we trust God and believe the promises of His Word during our storms of grief, pain, or persecution, we can be of good cheer. We can take heart. We can confidently proclaim, "The Lord is my helper. What can man do to me?"

As that Mediterranean storm raged around Paul and the frightened sailors, he continued to bring God's word. Things came to a crisis on the fourteenth night, when the ship neared land and the sailors feared it would be dashed apart on rocks. Paul encouraged the men, who had gone without food for two weeks, to eat:

> Wherefore I pray you to take some meat: for this is for your health: for there shall not an hair fall from the head of any of you. And when he had thus spoken, he took bread, and gave thanks to God in presence of them all: and when he had broken it, he began to eat. Then were they all of good cheer, and they also took some meat (vv. 34–36).

Paul again assured the men of God's care. None of them would go to a watery grave. In fact, the raging wind and sea would not rip even one hair from any of their heads! This language brings Matthew 10:30 to mind: God numbers every hair on our heads. Not one of them falls without His knowledge and permission.

The language in verse 35 mirrors that of the Lord's Supper. Paul took the bread and gave thanks to God. He broke it and began to eat. His sacramental action encouraged the fainting men. They took heart. They ate.

Do waves of anxiety wash over you? Does grief threaten to swamp your spirit? Has depression sunk your soul? Eat the bread of life. Drink deeply from the fountain of God's Word. Believe in your sovereign God and be of good cheer!

Questions for Reflection

What "ships" in my life ought to sink?

How can I be of good cheer and take rest even when "ship-wreck" threatens?

In what specific ways can I demonstrate good cheer to God and others today?

NO CONDEMNATION

22

Read: Romans 8

There is therefore now no condemnation to them which are in Christ Jesus, who walk not after the flesh, but after the Spirit…. What shall we then say to these things? If God be for us, who can be against us? He that spared not his own Son, but delivered him up for us all, how shall he not with him also freely give us all things? Who shall lay any thing to the charge of God's elect? It is God that justifieth. Who is he that condemneth? It is Christ that died, yea rather, that is risen again, who is even at the right hand of God, who also maketh intercession for us.

—ROMANS 8:1, 31–34

What Christian doesn't cherish Romans 8? From its stirring first verse to its rousing final line, the chapter sings truth after priceless truth. It revels in the beauties of life in the Spirit. It delights in the joy of our future glory. It proclaims God's wondrous love. It assures groaning believers of an interceding Spirit. It comforts Christians with a God who works all things for our good. And in it, God declares this verdict: not guilty!

The first verse of Romans 8 contains the important word "therefore." Whenever we see it in Scripture, we need to take the preceding text into consideration. In the previous section of Romans, Paul has shown that although Christians still struggle with sin, true believers no longer live under its domination. The Spirit helps us die more and more to sin while increasingly living for Christ.

Because this is true, those who walk in Christ's Spirit will not be condemned. Do we really comprehend this truth? "No condemnation" means *no condemnation*. It doesn't mean a tiny amount or a weakly pressed charge. It doesn't mean censure for one solitary sin. It means that Christ judges us not by our sin but by His own righteousness. This is one of those biblical doctrines that is easy to say. But knowing it in our heads is different from feeling it in our hearts.

If we believe this truth, it will affect the way we think and live. If Christ no longer condemns you, why worry when vindictive people denounce you? If He no longer condemns you, why judge yourself?

We rest in the Lord when the doctrine of no condemnation is assimilated emotionally. This comfort not only gives believers hope for glory, but it also sustains us in our current struggles. God's Spirit enables us to say with Paul: "For I reckon that the sufferings of this present time are not worthy to be compared with the glory which shall be revealed in us" (v. 18).

Can you grasp this? The ache of your grief, the chains of your chronic pain, and the trauma of your abuse cannot begin to compare with the inexpressible splendor that will be revealed in you—in your own glorified body. Your future is so immensely magnificent that your present suffering is not even worth comparing!

Still, this glorious future often seems far off. Sometimes we crawl along in the dust of this earth, groaning in our misery. But God's Spirit is our Great Interpreter:

Likewise the Spirit also helpeth our infirmities: for we know not what we should pray for as we ought: but the Spirit itself maketh intercession for us with groanings which cannot be uttered. And he that searcheth the hearts knoweth what is the mind of the Spirit, because he maketh intercession for the saints according to the will of God (vv. 26–27).

Even when our minds are too confused to formulate a prayer or our hearts ache too much to articulate a petition, the Spirit takes our incoherent moans and presents them to God in a way that pleases Him. God knows what is in our hearts. He and the Spirit are of one mind. The Spirit changes the deepest aching in our hearts into purified prayer.

Our most piercing pain often comes when we cannot understand why a loving heavenly Father would allow this horrible thing to happen to us or our loved ones. So many events make us cry out, "Why?" But God is sovereign: "And we know that all things work together for good to them that love God, to them who are the called according to his purpose" (v. 28). God orchestrates every event of our lives for our good and His glory. He doesn't promise good for unbelievers, but only for those He has called.

If you love God, *all* things work together for your good. It may be years before you see how some trial was for your good. You may never see it. But God has a purpose, and it is good. It's like the familiar analogy of a tapestry. God weaves threads together to form a beautiful scene, but we see only loose strands and tangled knots on the back. We walk by faith, not by sight (2 Cor. 5:7).

Our faith resides in a heavenly Father who loved us so much He gave us His own Son. If He gave this ultimate gift, we can trust Him to give us just what we need at just the right time (v. 32). If He is for us, who can be against us? (v. 31). Men may persecute, the devil may accuse, but no person or power can condemn the true believer. God has justified His elect through Christ, who died for our sins and now reigns at God's right hand (vv. 33–34).

No wonder Paul breaks into a marvelous doxology! Nothing can separate us from the love of our Lord and Savior Jesus Christ:

> Who shall separate us from the love of Christ? shall tribulation, or distress, or persecution, or famine, or nakedness, or peril, or sword? As it is written, For thy sake we are killed all the day long; we are accounted as sheep for the slaughter. Nay, in all these things we are more than conquerors through him that loved us. For I am persuaded, that neither death, nor life, nor angels, nor principalities, nor powers, nor things present, nor things to come, nor height, nor depth, nor any other creature, shall be able to separate us from the love of God, which is in Christ Jesus our Lord (vv. 35–39).

Amazing love indeed! Nothing, absolutely nothing, can separate you from the love of Christ. No prosperity or no adversity will ever move you from His love. Believers aren't wimps limping over life's trials. They are more than victorious warriors!

This is God's verdict for you: no condemnation. Are you persuaded? By grace, move this truth from your head to your heart. Believe it! Live it!

Questions for Reflection

Which of all these beautiful verses from Romans 8 speaks most to me? (Write it and memorize it.)

In what ways do I allow the devil, others, or myself to condemn me?

How do I need to act today to show I believe and rest in the truth of no condemnation?

23

SUFFICIENT GRACE

Read: 2 Corinthians 12

And he said unto me, My grace is sufficient for thee: for my strength is made perfect in weakness. Most gladly therefore will I rather glory in my infirmities, that the power of Christ may rest upon me. Therefore I take pleasure in infirmities, in reproaches, in necessities, in persecutions, in distresses for Christ's sake: for when I am weak, then am I strong.

—2 CORINTHIANS 12:9–10

If you've never really suffered, you're likely to skim over these verses from 2 Corinthians 12, thinking they express a nice sentiment. If you've been beyond despair or totally broken, you read these verses and weep. You recall your weakness. You know you survived that excruciating time only through Christ's strength and His power.

God's grace is indeed sufficient; He does manifest His strength in our weakness. But no one likes learning this lesson. Who wants to be weak and useless? We'd rather be self-confident and productive. Chronic pain saps our strength. Grief bows our spirits. Constant concerns burden as heavily as a permanent hundred-pound backpack. We reach the end of our physical strength, our emotional fortitude, and our mental capacity. We cry out, "Lord, I just can't do this any more! It's too much for me!"

It takes a lot to get us to that point. We're conditioned to doing our best and soldiering on. We hate admitting weaknesses. Who wants to be a wimp? But recognizing our limitations is the first step in dependence upon God.

Dependence carries negative connotations in our culture. We think of the wife who cannot go through one day without calling her husband ten times or the grown son who comes home nearly every day so Mom can do his laundry and fix his meals. Depending on the Lord, however, is positive and biblical. Far better to cry out to Him than muddle through on our own! Throwing ourselves in total trust upon the Lord opens our finite minds to comprehend His divine strength. You can't do it? Of course not! Whatever made you think you could? But you don't have to; He will.

The more we lean on God and trust Him, the more we see how amazingly He works through us. We are clay jars, cracked pots, but God fills us with His power. I marvel whenever God, in His inscrutable wisdom, chooses to use incredibly inept me.

Paul knew all about his own weakness and God's strength. He based his encouragement for fellow believers on his personal struggle. Whatever thorn penetrated his flesh, poisoning his system, he had begged God three times to remove it. Although God didn't take it away, He repeatedly promised sufficient grace.

Paul calls his thorn "the messenger of Satan" sent to "buffet" him (v. 7). Paul's thorn actively tormented him, but not without purpose. It humbled him, daily reminding him that he could do nothing apart from God's strength.

Even though continually pierced, Paul was able to glory in infirmities. Who can do that? Nothing seems less glorious than infirmity. Who can glory in weakness or illness, in being so incapacitated that others feed us and wash our bodies?

But Paul gladly glories in affliction because that is when he most feels Christ's presence. Infirmities are the vehicles God uses to propel His power. Paul goes so far as to say that he takes pleasure in infirmities, reproaches, necessities, and persecutions. I want to avoid reproaches and persecutions; I can't imagine enjoying them! Because these things make Paul weak, however, he more clearly feels God's strength. He views them as first-person encounters with God.

Writing these devotional reflections stretched me beyond my limits and brought me to my knees. My deadlines for this and other work seemed impossible. Personal concerns overwhelmed me. Negative thoughts discouraged me. Peace eluded me. I wrested out each reluctant word. Rarely had I felt such strong spiritual attack.

I ruefully recognized the irony of feeling stressed and depressed while trying to write about resting in the Lord. I begged friends and family to pray for me. For two weeks, nothing changed, except the appearance of a genuinely impossible deadline. The next day, something happened that I cannot explain. I had a good day.

It was filled with such peace and productivity that it almost terrified me. I realized how very far it was from my normal experience. I was afraid I'd never have another, and I very much wanted to. I wanted to think the magic thought, say the magic word, or do the magic trick to make these kinds of days miraculously appear.

But I couldn't make it happen. It was God's miracle. His grace suffused my soul. More than sufficient, it surged in joyful waves of abundance. I had known that God's grace was sufficient, but I suddenly felt it.

Certainly I'd been writing these devotionals as much (or more!) for my own benefit as anyone else's. Perhaps truth finally penetrated my thick skull. Perhaps my entire psyche realized that everything I was trying to do was truly impossible, and even my subconscious mind finally turned it all over to the Lord. The only thing I know for sure is that my weakness displayed God's power.

My days aren't all peachy peace and creamy productivity. As I type, I'm actually behind my self-imposed schedule. But I rest more often in God and His sufficient grace.

In Paul's letter to the Corinthians, he asked: "And who is sufficient for these things?" (2 Cor. 2:16). He answered: "Not that we are sufficient of ourselves to think any thing as of ourselves; but our sufficiency is of God" (2 Cor. 3:5). We can do nothing in our own strength; God does it all. Later in this same letter, Paul wrote: "For though he was crucified through weakness, yet he liveth by the power of God. For we also are weak in him, but we shall live with him by the power of God toward you" (2 Cor. 13:4).

The astounding power that raised Jesus from the dead is the same power living within those who are in Christ! That power will surge in your weakest moment. It will invigorate you to your earthly tasks. And it will take your soul to your heavenly home and revive your dead body at Christ's return. God's grace truly is sufficient!

Questions for Reflection

Am I allowing the thorns that prick my flesh to poison my system, or remind me to lean on God?

Where am I finding my sufficiency?

In what specific ways can I show today that I am resting in God and His grace is sufficient for me?

OUR PEACE

24

Read: Ephesians 2

But now in Christ Jesus ye who sometimes were far off are made nigh by the blood of Christ. For he is our peace, who hath made both one, and hath broken down the middle wall of partition between us; having abolished in his flesh the enmity, even the law of commandments contained in ordinances; for to make in himself of twain one new man, so making peace; and that he might reconcile both unto God in one body by the cross, having slain the enmity thereby: and came and preached peace to you which were afar off, and to them that were nigh. For through him we both have access by one Spirit unto the Father.
—EPHESIANS 2:13–18

What is your definition of "peace"? Some people may immediately think of a Middle East truce, a country free from warfare, or safe city streets. Others may envision tranquility in nature, harmony in the home, or serenity in the soul.

Have you ever defined Christ as your peace? Ephesians 2:14 does. Christ is the peace treaty between Jew and Gentile. He is the slayer of the enmity dragon that came between God and man (v. 16).

When Adam succumbed to Satan's temptation, he lost fellowship with God. He and all his descendants became God's enemies instead of His friends. But God made a promise. Even though the serpent would strike the heel of the woman's offspring, this holy seed would crush Satan's head (Gen 3:15). God set apart the Jewish nation as His chosen ones and entered into a special relationship with His people, teaching them through ritual and prophecy about that Messiah: "But he was wounded for our transgressions, he was bruised for our iniquities: the chastisement of our peace was upon him; and with his stripes we are healed" (Isa. 53:5). The Suffering Servant bore the punishment of our peace and became our peace.

Jesus came to preach peace to the Samaritan woman as well as the Jewish rabbi; He came for those who were far off and those who were near (v. 17). His death on the cross ripped the veil and razed the wall. He reconciled God to man, both Jews and Gentiles. Believers who were once God's enemies are now His friends. Ephesians 2:18 proclaims this trinitarian truth: we come to the Father by the Spirit through the Son.

All believers were once dead in sin, walking in worldly ways, subject to the prince of ethereal power (v. 2). But God's grace vivified us; we became subjects of the Prince of eternal Peace (Isa. 9:6). God did this out of His rich mercy and great love:

> But God, who is rich in mercy, for his great love where-
> with he loved us, even when we were dead in sins, hath
> quickened us together with Christ, (by grace ye are
> saved;).... For by grace are ye saved through faith; and
> that not of yourselves: it is the gift of God: not of works,
> lest any man should boast (vv. 4–5, 8–9).

God saves believers by grace and through faith. Salvation is not something we can initiate, facilitate, or finish. It is not partly God and partly us; it is all God from first to last (Rom. 1:17). We cannot boast about our role in salvation because it does not depend in any way on our works.

We see God's mercy in His gracious work of salvation, but someday we will see even more of His rich grace: "And hath raised us up together, and made us sit together in heavenly places in Christ Jesus: that in the ages to come he might shew the exceeding riches of his grace in his kindness toward us through Christ Jesus" (vv. 6–7). God has already raised us up to sit in heavenly places with Christ. This knowledge is "too wonderful for me" (Ps. 139:6). In some way beyond our understanding, we are already seated with Christ in heaven. And in the endless ages of the future, we will experience the limitless riches of God's grace and kindness through Christ.

Scriptural construction is often instructive. Note that the section emphasizing God's grace in salvation, apart from our works, is followed with this gem: "For we are his workmanship, created in Christ Jesus unto good works, which God hath before ordained that we should walk in them" (v. 10).

The ultimate artist, our Creator God, crafts each believer as His masterpiece. Earthly artists imitate God's creativity when they produce a beautiful painting, sculpture, novel, or sonnet. But like a lovely goblet, we have been created for a purpose: to do the good works that God has ordained for us before our birth. Our good works are possible only through Christ Jesus. They do not earn salvation but rather are an inherent product of it.

There is no clashing in the composition of God's symphony. It displays balance and harmony. His masterpiece is a beautifully constructed temple:

> Now therefore ye are no more strangers and foreigners,
> but fellowcitizens with the saints, and of the household
> of God; and are built upon the foundation of the apos-
> tles and prophets, Jesus Christ himself being the chief
> corner stone; in whom all the building fitly framed
> together groweth unto an holy temple in the Lord: in
> whom ye also are builded together for an habitation of
> God through the Spirit (vv. 19–22).

Built on the foundation of the apostles and prophets, with Christ as the cornerstone, every stone joins together into a harmonious whole. This trinitarian temple is built on the Son, through the Spirit, for the Father. The church reflects triune unity: believers live in the Spirit, under a leadership that submits to Christ, to the glory of God.

When we walk together in the works God has ordained for us, we experience peace within our congregations. Our peace as a local church and the universal church comes through Christ. He is our collective peace as well as our personal peace.

When His peace pervades our hearts, we live in unity with fellow believers. We worship corporately as one body, hearing His word proclaimed in the Spirit. And when we begin to comprehend the remarkable truth of Christ as our own peace, we begin to develop a daily attitude of Sabbath rest.

Questions for Reflection

What does it mean to me that Christ is my peace?

How does the knowledge that I am already seated with Christ in heaven color my daily attitude?

How will I rest in God today as His masterpiece and part of His holy temple?

25

CONSTANT CONTENTMENT

Read: Philippians 4

I have learned, in whatsoever state I am, therewith to be content.... But my God shall supply all your need according to his riches in glory by Christ Jesus. —PHILIPPIANS 4:11, 19

Like Jeremiah Burroughs, who wrote *The Rare Jewel of Christian Contentment* in 1648, you may find contentment difficult to dig up. Unearthing this uncommon gem requires sifting through layers of self-seeking sediment. This is difficult to do occasionally, and nearly impossible to do continually. But as Paul sat in prison, he wrote in Philippians 4 of being constantly content. He knew what it was to be abased or to abound, to be well fed or hungry, to live in abundance or to suffer need (v. 12). He had completed an intensive course in contentment training.

This is what Paul learned as the prerequisite for being content everywhere and in everything: "I can do all things through Christ which strengtheneth me" (v. 13). Paul rested contentedly in God. Christ supplied the strength he needed for every circumstance and situation. Christ called him to his tasks and equipped him for them.

This verse doesn't support a workaholic or people-pleaser mentality. When Paul writes "all things," he means all things God calls him to do, not all things we think we should do or all things everyone else wants us to do. He means depending on God and resting in Christ through all our physical, mental, and emotional states. He means trusting God to supply, not everything we *want*, but everything we *need* to accomplish His will.

Since Paul has learned to trust God for his every need, he confidently asserts that God will do the same for the believers in Philippi. God's provision will not be stingy but rather will be bountiful, "according to his riches in glory by Christ Jesus" (v. 19).

In whatever trial we find ourselves, God will provide just what we need from the abundance of Christ. Through Him, we can meet our deadlines or meet the school bus. We can change careers or change diapers. We can cope with infertility or live with the loss of a child. We have strength to stand by the gaping grave of a longtime spouse or survive the agonizing treatments of cancer. Christ's strength carries us through depression's numbness, anxiety's storm, or interminable nights of flaming pain.

Paul's relationship with the Philippians was one of reciprocal love and support. He taught them well, and they supported him well. In loving language, he encourages them to stand firm in the Lord (v. 1). He rejoices with them in their opportunity to express their concern and kindness. He exults that their gift demonstrates abundant fruit (v. 17) and pleases God like a fragrant offering (v. 18).

Joy characterizes the entire book of Philippians, typified by Paul's imperative: "Rejoice in the Lord always: and again I say, Rejoice" (v. 4). Being joyful all the time seems almost as difficult as being constantly content, but the two commands are intrinsically related. This joy is not a happy-clappy giddiness, but a deeply rooted assurance of God's continual care.

Because God cares for us and gives us every good and perfect gift, we need not be anxious about anything. We can lay our cares and concerns before God's heavenly throne in prayer and supplication with thanksgiving (v. 6). When you find yourself becoming anxious or worried, stop that thought process. Instead of mentally screaming for help, think of things for which you can thank God.

You will soon find panic replaced with peace: "And the peace of God, which passeth all understanding, shall keep your hearts and minds through Christ Jesus" (v. 7). The peace of God truly is beyond all human understanding. It fills one's spirit with an almost luminous tranquility. God's remarkable peace preserves our hearts and our minds through our union with Christ Jesus. Should arthritis cripple our fingers or Parkinson's weaken our legs, should Alzheimer's steal our memories or dementia befuddle our brains, that inherent part of us called the soul remains secure in Christ.

Depending on Christ's strength is the key to contentment with its resulting joy, thankfulness, and peace. A spiritually positive attitude can unlock the leg chains that drag us down and slow our progress. Paul recommends that his Philippian brothers and sisters give careful attention to the types of things they allow to dwell in their minds: "Finally, brethren, whatsoever things are true, whatsoever things are honest, whatsoever things are just, whatsoever things are pure, whatsoever things are lovely, whatsoever things are of good report; if there be any virtue, and if there be any praise, think on these things" (v. 8).

Paul is the original proponent of positive thinking, but not the way it is preached by some in our day. Long before the development of cognitive therapy in psychology, Paul promoted the practice of restructured thinking. He urged believers to banish negative thoughts by filling their minds with things that are true, honest, just, pure, lovely, of good report, virtuous, and praiseworthy. How little of modern media falls into any of these categories! We ought to reassess the music we listen to, the movies we view, the TV programs we watch, the Internet sites we visit, and the books we read. Begin by opening your mind to the good. Continue by replacing negative thoughts or images with positive and spiritually edifying ones.

We sometimes dwell on how busy we are and how little we seem to accomplish, which leads us to feel as if we're spinning our wheels. Instead, try to think about the positives of your situation. "Yes, homeschooling eats my time like a ravenous beast, but I'm thankful for this opportunity to have a lifelong impact in my children's lives"; or, "Yes, the trauma from abuse damaged me and my relationships on multiple levels, but I'm thankful that my Redeemer is slowly and surely healing me." Take time today to evaluate your own negative thinking habits.

Contentment is indeed a rare jewel; constant contentment is as rare as a blue diamond. But by God's grace, we can learn to be content by relying on Christ's strength and rejoicing in all our circumstances, coupling supplication with thanksgiving and thinking about praiseworthy things.

Determine today to dig beneath your layers of selfishness and pride to uncover this rare and most precious gem: contentment!

Questions for Reflection

In what areas today do I need to depend more on Christ's strength and less on my own?

In what ways do I need to change my thoughts and prayers?

How can I rest in Christ today by filling my mind with positive and edifying thoughts or images?

26

GOD'S PEACE

Read: Colossians 3

And let the peace of God rule in your hearts, to the which also ye are called in one body; and be ye thankful.

—COLOSSIANS 3:15

In this chapter of Colossians, Paul expands positive thinking (Phil. 4:8) to encompass positive living. Even though believers have been regenerated by the Holy Spirit and no longer live under sin's control, they still struggle against persistent sin. Colossians 3 helps us understand how to renew our lives and relationships.

Before Paul gets into the specifics, he tells Christians why they should: "If ye then be risen with Christ, seek those things which are above, where Christ sitteth on the right hand of God. Set your affection on things above, not on things on the earth. For ye are dead, and your life is hid with Christ in God" (vv. 1–3).

Believers have already been raised with Christ, who sits at the right hand of God. This language echoes the truth of Ephesians 2:6, which is beyond our comprehension. But our union with Christ enables us to seek and set our minds on things above rather than on earthly desires. Because we have died and our lives are hidden with Christ in God, we will one day appear with Christ, who is our life, in His glory (v. 4). Since God guarantees this glorious future for Christians, we wage our present warfare with hope. In Christ, we have the power to slay the evil desires that characterized us before we were saved.

Don't skim over the lists in verses 5 and 8 too quickly. You may think you're living a chaste life, but what about immoral thoughts or desires? Also, few people are immune from coveting. Perhaps you think you're only admiring your friend's new Sunday clothes, your neighbor's new car, or your relative's comfortable home, but our admiration often contains traces of covetousness. And God declares that coveting is idolatry, which is putting our desire for anything above our desire for God. What about anger? Everyone gets angry sometimes. We may fool ourselves into thinking that our anger is righteous, like Jesus cleansing the temple, but does our anger flow from hearts distraught over God's glory? Or from hearts seeking our own glory? Consider your speech. Almost without noticing, gossip, slander, and obscenities slip from our lips.

At the end of Paul's listings of sins to be slain, he writes: "Lie not one to another, seeing that ye have put off the old man with his deeds; and have put on the new man, which is renewed in knowledge after the image of him that created him" (vv. 9–10).

Paul emphasizes the sin of lying by placing it in the final position of prominence and power. This exhortation signals an approaching extension. He will show that sin's personal death in our bodies has great ramifications for corporate life in the body.

But first Paul urges believers to put off the old self and put on the new one. That language conveys something we do, like changing clothes. We discard our old selfish rags and clothe ourselves in new selfless attire. The words also imply continued action. Even clean clothes get stained and dirty if we don't change out of them and wash them. We must monitor our hearts and minds daily to put on fresh garments of godly living.

Putting on the new self means being renewed increasingly in the image of our Creator God (v. 10). When all believers renew themselves after God's image, divisions within the church disappear. Ethnic, cultural, geographical, and class cliques vanish. "Christ is all, and in all" (v. 11).

God commands His chosen people, whom He loves and considers holy, to have compassionate hearts that express kindness, humility, meekness, and patience. We are to bear with one another and forgive each other, remembering how much our Lord has forgiven us. Above all these things, we must wrap ourselves in love, which binds everything together in perfect harmony (v. 14). Love is the golden thread that sews the pieces of the new-self cloth into one harmonious garment. Within the discussion of individual change for communal benefit, our focus verse (v. 15) calls us to let the peace of God rule our hearts as one body and to be thankful.

The imperative "let" indicates that we can play a role in allowing God's peace to dwell in our hearts. Things we do might prevent peace; disobeying God or living in discord with fellow believers deters peace. Setting our minds on things above and loving others promote peace. Peace comes from God. We can't create His peace within us, but we can think and live in ways that open our hearts wider to receive it. To let the peace of God rule in our hearts is a communal command for the entire body. When individual believers allow God's peace to guide their emotions and behavior, God's peace reigns throughout the body of Christ.

Notice that our focus verse concludes with a command we've seen before: to be thankful. Thankfulness ought to characterize the Christian mind. A grateful spirit that frequently thanks God for His blessings generates a peace-filled heart.

The word of Christ forms the basis for our relationships in the church and home:

> Let the word of Christ dwell in you richly in all wisdom; teaching and admonishing one another in psalms and hymns and spiritual songs, singing with grace in your hearts to the Lord. And whatsoever ye do in word or deed, do all in the name of the Lord Jesus, giving thanks to God and the Father by him (vv. 16–17).

Christ's words create wisdom. Godly wisdom overflows in godly teaching, admonishing, and singing with grateful praise. We keep our focus in relationships and work by remembering that everything we do is for the glory of Christ's name. After several specific guidelines for relationships in verses 18–22, Paul reiterates that believers should do every task "heartily, as to the Lord, and not unto men," assuring them that those who serve Christ will be rewarded with an inheritance (vv. 23–24).

Because our life is hidden in the risen Christ, we're able to discard the old self's filthy rags and daily don the new self's clean apparel. When individual believers are increasingly renewed in God's image, His peace pervades the body of Christ. Let the peace of God rule your heart! May the word of Christ dwell in you richly and wisely!

Questions for Reflection

How does knowing I'm raised with Christ change the focus of my thoughts and pursuits today?

What old-self rags cling to me, and how can I replace them with new-self garments?

What can I do today to find rest by letting God's peace rule my heart and Christ's word dwell in me richly?

27

SOUND MIND

Read: 2 Timothy 1

For God hath not given us the spirit of fear; but of power, and of love, and of a sound mind.
—2 TIMOTHY 1:7

My friend Karen claimed 2 Timothy 1:7 as her theme verse when she climbed to Mt. Everest's base camp with other cancer survivors in April of 2011. Karen likes staying home with her family or spending time with familiar friends. She doesn't like being cold. The idea of flying halfway around the world, into the world's most dangerous airport, then trekking with strangers across primitive suspension bridges and miles of mountainous terrain in the bitter cold, filled her with a spirit of fear. But she trusted God. Stretched beyond her limits, God strengthened her faith and generated new friendships through His spirit of power, love, and a sound mind.

We may not have such extraordinary opportunities to put this verse's truth to the test, but we all face struggles and demands that pull us outside our comfort zones. Our bodies and minds scream in protest while our hearts fill with panic. But that isn't the spirit God has given us. His Spirit produces physical strength, emotional stability, and mental soundness. Fear may visit the true Christian, but it shouldn't take up permanent residence.

True faith banishes fear and fosters fellowship. This first chapter of 2 Timothy portrays a model of Christian companionship. Paul's love for Timothy and Timothy's concern for him generated continual prayer for each other. They wept together in each other's struggles, and each delighted in the other's joy (vv. 3–4). Paul was sure that Timothy, like his grandmother and mother, had sincere faith. He called it "unfeigned faith" (v. 5).

There is such a thing as feigned faith. Jesus warns us about false prophets, wolves in sheep's clothing. He teaches us to recognize them by their fruits, saying:

> Not every one that saith unto me, Lord, Lord, shall enter into the kingdom of heaven; but he that doeth the will of my Father which is in heaven. Many will say to me in that day, Lord, Lord, have we not prophesied in thy name? and in thy name have cast out devils? and in thy name done many wonderful works? And then will I profess unto them, I never knew you: depart from me, ye that work iniquity (Matt. 7:21–23).

These false prophets pray, "Lord, Lord" and do amazing good deeds in Christ's name. They are powerful preachers! But there is a discrepancy between their public and private lives. An apple may appear firm and red, but inside it is mushy and brown. Rotten fruit indicates false faith.

True faith produces sound fruit and a sound mind. Faith does not exempt believers from mental distresses or disorders, but it does ground their thinking in Christ. Some Bible versions translate "sound mind" as "self-control." The way we think influences the way we act. A clear mind focused on Christ leads to selfless service for Christ and others. A muddled mind that justifies sin results in self-service that indulges in perverted personal desires.

Timothy's gift came from the laying on of Paul's hands when he was ordained to ministry, but the Holy Spirit's work isn't limited only to pastors. A minister is a servant, and we are all servants of Christ. The Holy Spirit is a gift to all believers, a gift Paul tells us to "stir up," which other versions translate as "fan into flame" (v. 6 ESV). We shouldn't become so paralyzed by fear that we allow the Spirit's fire to smolder as dark embers. We ought to stir up those coals and fan them into roaring flames!

That is exercising our God-given spirit of power, love, and a sound mind. We will be enabled to proclaim the testimony of our Lord without shame and to participate in the afflictions of the gospel with the power of God (v. 8).

By His power, God called us to salvation by grace:

> Who hath saved us, and called us with an holy calling, not according to our works, but according to his own purpose and grace, which was given us in Christ Jesus before the world began, but is now made manifest by the appearing of our Saviour Jesus Christ, who hath abolished death, and hath brought life and immortality to light through the gospel (vv. 9–10).

Before God laid the foundation of the earth (Job 38:4), He elected us by grace and according to His purpose. God's plan of salvation was revealed through Christ's perfectly obedient life and His perfectly atoning death, which brought us eternal security. This good news shines as the gospel light in a dark world.

Paul suffered for the gospel cause. Yet he was not ashamed:

> For the which cause I also suffer these things: neverthe-
> less I am not ashamed: for I know whom I have believed,
> and am persuaded that he is able to keep that which I
> have committed unto him against that day. Hold fast
> the form of sound words, which thou has heard of me,
> in faith and love which is in Christ Jesus. That good
> thing which was committed unto thee keep by the Holy
> Ghost which dwelleth in us (vv. 12–14).

God gives the Holy Spirit to believers as a guarantee of full
and eternal salvation. Paul was not ashamed because he
knew the gospel was true and his salvation was secure.

He propounds in 2 Timothy not only the doctrines of
salvation by grace and predestination, but also persever-
ance (or better, preservation) of the saints. True believers
don't have to worry about losing their faith. God will keep
it secure until the final day.

Paul exhorts believers to "hold fast the form of sound
words...in faith and love" (v. 13). Biblical teachings are
sound words for those who by genuine faith truly love
Christ and the members of His church. Examine the root
of faith in your heart and the fruit of faith in your life. Are
they genuine? If you truly believe, be fully persuaded that
you can never lose your salvation. God the Holy Spirit lives
within you and guarantees it.

Like the apostle Paul and Daniel Whittle (who wrote
the words to the hymn "I Know Not Why God's Wondrous
Grace"), I know whom I have believed, and am persuaded
that He is able to keep that which I've committed unto Him
against that day.

Scripture's sound words shape a sound mind centered on Christ. Chase the spirit of fear from your heart by fanning the embers of God's Spirit into a roaring flame!

Questions for Reflection

If I genuinely examine the root and fruit of my faith, is it unfeigned?

How can I rest in God by fanning into flame the gift of the Holy Spirit in a sound mind?

In what specific ways can I demonstrate genuine faith through love for others today?

ENTER REST

28

Read: Hebrews 3:7–4:16

To day if ye will hear his voice, harden not your hearts....
There remaineth therefore a rest to the people of God. For
he that is entered into his rest, he also hath ceased from his
own works, as God did from his. Let us labour therefore to
enter into that rest, lest any man fall after the same example
of unbelief.
—HEBREWS 4:7, 9–11

This section of Hebrews gathers threads about rest from throughout the entire Bible and ties them together into one secure knot that cannot unravel. It shows God's creation ordinance of rest and His people entering the rest of the Promised Land. We see rest rooted in true faith, evidenced by obedience. We see the hope for our eternal rest. And we see Christ our Redeemer, who understands our human frailties because He lived as a man, interceding for us as our Great High Priest.

After speaking about the superiority of Christ, first to prophets and angels and then to Moses, the writer of Hebrews warns against hardened hearts like those of the Israelites. Because their hearts were hard, they failed to trust God, and so they wandered forty more years in the wilderness. Under Joshua, they finally listened to the Lord's promises and entered the Promised Land. The author of Hebrews warns readers three times against failing to hear God and hardening their hearts (Heb. 3:7–8, 15; 4:7).

Mark Buchanan notes these repetitions in his excellent *The Rest of God: Restoring Your Soul by Restoring Sabbath* and reflects: "Here's the paradox: If we don't listen, we never enter his rest. Yet if we don't enter his rest, we never listen" (p. 188). Listening to God comprises a primary component of rest. God commands: "Be still, and know that I am God" (Ps. 46:10). Only when we cease frantic thoughts and activities can we still our spirits to hear God's whispers in today's whirlwinds.

In his commentary on this part of Hebrews, John Calvin describes how the author of Hebrews connects the rest of the Promised Land with our eternal, as well as our daily rest: "He draws the conclusion, that there is a sabbathizing reserved for God's people, that is, a spiritual rest; to which God daily invites us" (4:9). Sabbath rest is a day set apart, a foretaste of our eternal rest, but it is also a daily attitude of trusting God and resting in Him; it encompasses continued belief in His promises, thankful prayer for His merciful grace, and careful listening to His word.

Did you pause when you read the command in Hebrews 4:1 to fear? This verse harks back to Exodus 20:20 (see day 3), when Moses told the people to "fear not," for God was testing them so they would fear Him and not sin. A proper awe and reverence for God generates obedience. God has promised His people everlasting rest, but a disobedient life evidences an unbelieving heart. We who have God's written Word hear Him speak more clearly than the Israelites did, who heard it directly from Moses, but they didn't truly listen because their faith wasn't genuine (v. 2).

Hebrews 4:3–4 contrasts the hope of rest for believers with the impossibility of rest for unbelievers. It then couples that contrast with God's resting after creating the foundation of the world, which brings to mind our reflection on Genesis 2:2–3 (day 1).

The author of Hebrews reasons that since God promised His rest and the Israelites didn't enter due to their unbelief, His promise still remains for believers (vv. 5–9). The allusion to David in verse 7 refers to Psalm 95:7–8, which is quoted in the last part of the verse: "To day if ye will hear his voice, harden not your hearts."

On whatever day the original recipients of Hebrews read this, they were exhorted to hear God's voice and soften their hearts. On whatever day all the people since have read it, they too are urged to listen and soften their hearts. As I write this, I am commanded to allow God's words to penetrate any hardness in my heart. As you read this, you are encouraged to open your ears and your heart.

God promises rest to those who cease from works, just as God did. We must rest from evil deeds and strive toward attentive faith (vv. 10–11).

Note God's Word carefully: "For the word of God is quick, and powerful, and sharper than any twoedged sword, piercing even to the dividing asunder of soul and spirit, and of the joints and marrow, and is a discerner of the thoughts and intents of the heart" (v. 12). God's Word lives. It is powerful. Sharper than a rapier, it pierces your very soul. God's Spirit discerns every thought and intent of your heart. What implications this has for how we view personal Bible reading as well as Sunday sermons! We become even more uncomfortable when we realize that no one can hide from God (Ps. 139:7–15). We stand naked before Him, and He sees all our sins (v. 13).

But don't give up! We are clothed with the righteousness of Christ, our Great High Priest in heaven: "Seeing then that we have a great high priest, that is passed into the heavens, Jesus the Son of God, let us hold fast our profession" (v. 14). Believers are urged to take hold of their profession and grasp it with both hands. We can do this because our salvation is secure in Christ. He has gone to heaven to prepare a place for all who believe in Him and live for Him.

Still we struggle. We sink under the weight of pain. We fall into the allure of sin. But our High Priest understands our every trial:

> For we have not an high priest which cannot be touched with the feeling of our infirmities; but was in all points tempted like as we are, yet without sin. Let us therefore come boldly unto the throne of grace, that we may obtain mercy, and find grace to help in time of need (vv. 15–16).

Jesus Christ lived as a man on this earth. He had a real body and human emotions. He completely understands our frailties and our feelings. He was like us in every way except sin. He was hungry, lonely, humiliated, and betrayed. He knows.

Christ, our High Priest, sits at the right hand of God, interceding for us in our need. With Him there, pleading our cause before the Father, we can come before the throne of grace without fear or timidity. We can be bold!

Listen to God's voice today. Hear His promises of rest with a softened heart. Grip those promises and live in a way that demonstrates your faith. Pray boldly!

Questions for Reflection

Am I listening to God today and every day?

How am I striving to enter God's rest?

What can I do today to show that I really believe God's promise of eternal rest?

29

NEVER LEAVE

Read: Hebrews 13

Let your conversation be without covetousness; and be content with such things as ye have: for he hath said, I will never leave thee, nor forsake thee. So that we may boldly say, The Lord is my helper, and I will not fear what man shall do unto me.

—HEBREWS 13:5–6

Tucked within the treasure chest of guidelines for Christian living that comprises Hebrews 13, familiar gems glint. In the first part of verse 5, the author of Hebrews urges believers to live without covetousness and to be content. The warning against covetousness reminds us of Jesus' teaching in Luke 12 (day 19), as well as Paul's listing of sins in Colossians 3 (day 26). The encouragement toward contentment recalls Paul's confession in Philippians 4:11: "I have learned, in whatsoever state I am, therewith to be content" (day 25).

Hebrews 13:5 urges believers to be content with what they have. When we think about what we have, rather than what we don't have, thankfulness replaces envy and gratitude crowds out covetousness. Focusing on who we are and what we have in Christ helps us realize that having Christ, we have everything.

The same verse goes on to reiterate God's promise to be with His people always. This reminds us of Deuteronomy 31 and Joshua 1, when Joshua took the reins of leadership from Moses to lead the Israelites into the Promised Land.

Some scholars believe this quote comes from Joshua, but in his commentary on this passage of Hebrews John Calvin writes, "I am rather of the opinion that it is a sentence drawn from the common doctrine of Scripture, as though he had said, 'The Lord everywhere promises that he will never be wanting to us'" (13:5). We can agree with Calvin when we consider that, during this month of Sundays, we've glimpsed how God's promise always to be with us permeates Scripture. Jesus Himself promised to be with us always, until the very end of the age (Matt. 28:20).

Verse 6 also proclaims a truth found throughout the Bible, quoting from Psalm 118:6: "The LORD is on my side; I will not fear: what can man do unto me?" If the almighty God of heaven is on our side as our great helper, why would we fear a mere mortal? Why be afraid of what other people think? The lies they spread? Or even their destructive and evil deeds? God holds believers in His hands; nothing or no one can snatch us from His firm grip (John 10:28–29).

These are just some of the gems appearing in Hebrews 13, which begins, "Let brotherly love continue" and provides exhortations to foster faith and fellowship. Brotherly love binds believers together in Christian community. Love for God and others squelches the self-promotion that wrecks havoc within the home or a church family. Love covers a multitude of sins (1 Peter 4:8).

Part of living in congregational harmony is a proper relationship between church members and their leaders: "Obey them that have the rule over you, and submit yourselves: for they watch for your souls, as they that must give account, that they may do it with joy, and not with grief: for that is unprofitable for you" (v. 17).

Church members are called to submit willingly to their leaders in everything that accords with God's will. This is not only so that the leaders' work will be joyful instead of filled with grief but also to the profit of those under their leadership. Church leaders have a huge responsibility. This text stresses the seriousness of their spiritual oversight by stating that they must guard the flock's very souls. More than that, they will eventually be required to give an account for their care.

Loving every member in our church and willingly submitting to our leaders may not always be easy, but it is possible because both members and leaders are under the authority of Christ, who does not change: "Jesus Christ the same yesterday, and to day, and for ever" (v. 8). Christ's constancy and the stability of God's Word keep Christians on course when buffeted by the winds of new or strange doctrines. God's grace, rather than empty ritual, forms the foundation of our faith (v. 9).

All the sacrifices in the Old Testament never removed one sin; they only pointed to Christ, who removed them all for those who believe. The blood of those sacrificial animals was brought into the sanctuary, but the bodies were burned outside the camp. Just so, Jesus died outside the city (vv. 11–12). We are called to bear Christ's reproach (v. 13) and leave the city that is not our home:

> For here have we no continuing city, but we seek one
> to come. By him therefore let us offer the sacrifice of

praise to God continually, that is, the fruit of our lips giving thanks to his name. But to do good and to communicate forget not: for with such sacrifices God is well pleased (vv. 14–16).

This isn't the first time the author of Hebrews has written about believers longing for the heavenly city (11:16; 12:22). The city we long to inhabit is eternal, in contrast to this world's temporal city of man. As we live outside the city of man, in the company of Christ and within the city of God, we offer a continual sacrifice of thankful praise. We shouldn't neglect to do good or to share what we have, for these sacrifices please God. He does not desire a bloody or burnt carcass, but a broken spirit and a contrite heart. He will not despise such offerings (Ps. 51:16–17).

The expansive benediction near the end of Hebrews 13 fills believers' hearts with God's peace:

Now the God of peace, that brought again from the dead our Lord Jesus, that great shepherd of the sheep, through the blood of the everlasting covenant, make you perfect in every good work to do his will, working in you that which is wellpleasing in his sight, through Jesus Christ; to whom be glory for ever and ever. Amen (vv. 20–21).

The God of peace will never leave us or forsake us. He raised the Great Shepherd from the dead through the blood of His everlasting covenant. In having Him, we have everything! Filled with grateful thanks, our humble and contrite hearts become a pleasing sacrifice. Jesus Christ works in us and will perfect us one day. All for His glory!

Questions for Reflection

If I am convinced that God will never leave me, how will that help me put to rest my fears?

Does my attitude toward my church leaders cause them joy or grief?

In what specific ways can I live today as a fragrant offering to God?

30

ETERNAL GLORY

Read: 1 Peter 5

Casting all your care upon him; for he careth for you.... But the God of all grace, who hath called us unto his eternal glory by Christ Jesus, after that ye have suffered a while, make you perfect, stablish, strengthen, settle you.
—1 PETER 5:7, 10

One of my favorite texts in all Scripture appears in 1 Peter 5. Despite having read the chapter numerous times, I confess that—until I wrote this reflection—I didn't realize that verse 7 so closely follows instructions to elders for shepherding God's flock. Studying this verse in context enhances my respect for those God calls to provide oversight in His church, as well as my awareness of their weighty responsibility.

The apostle Peter, who learned directly from Christ and witnessed His sufferings firsthand, exhorts elders to "feed the flock of God which is among you, taking the oversight thereof, not by constraint, but willingly; not for filthy lucre, but of a ready mind; neither as being lords over God's heritage, but being examples to the flock" (vv. 2–3).

Elders bear a heavy load! They first must see to it that the flock under their care is being regularly fed God's true word. They also need to feed the flock in their personal interaction with its members, during times of illness or death as well as when admonition becomes necessary. They should not have their arms twisted to accept the office but must serve willingly. Teaching elders or ministers receive a salary but must never be in ministry for financial gain. This warning is against more than money. Paid or not, pastors and elders should never seek self-promotion. They bear Christ's authority and must always strive for His glory. All elders ought to perform their work eagerly. They may never be domineering, leading instead by example.

These are high standards, but the godly pastor or elder will receive a crown of glory when Christ, the Chief Shepherd, returns (v. 4). All church leaders and members of the congregation are united under His final authority.

Because the word "elder" in verse 5 is contrasted with those who are "younger," its meaning appears to change from the previous references to those holding church office to those who are actually older in age. Since this verse also speaks of "all of you," these instructions seem to indicate a more inclusive audience.

The immediate context for our first focus verse occurs within an exhortation for all believers to practice mutual humility:

> Yea, all of you be subject one to another, and be clothed with humility: for God resisteth the proud, and giveth grace to the humble. Humble yourselves therefore under the mighty hand of God, that he may exalt you in due time: casting all your care upon him; for he careth for you (vv. 5–7).

Humility should be the believer's garment. All members of a church fellowship ought to be willing to put aside their own agendas and promote the welfare of others.

None should think themselves better than others. Nothing should be done out of selfish ambition or conceit, but all should esteem others as better than themselves (Phil. 2:3). Submitting to each other and to our church leaders is really submission to God. If we humble ourselves under His mighty hand, He will exalt us eventually. Our elevation may not come as quickly as we'd like, but it will happen in God's perfect time.

Within the same sentence as Peter's injunction to humble ourselves under God's hand and wait patiently for our future exaltation, he assures believers: "Casting all your care upon him; for he careth for you" (v. 7). Does it initially seem a bit strange to link humility with giving over cares to God? Knowing that God controls all the events of our lives and cares for us enables us to cast our concerns upon Him. It also helps us submit humbly and patiently to others and to God's will. When we trust in God's providence, we can rest in His love.

Lest his reader take this wonderful promise as license for apathy, Peter warns, "Be sober, be vigilant; because your adversary the devil, as a roaring lion, walketh about, seeking whom he may devour: whom resist stedfast in the faith, knowing that the same afflictions are accomplished in your brethren that are in the world" (vv. 8–9).

The devil can prowl like a roaring lion or appear as an angel of light (2 Cor. 11:14). We do well to be on guard for both manifestations. He is never satisfied; he always seeks more flesh to tear, more lives to devour. We resist him by remaining firm in our faith, knowing that we're not alone in our struggles. Christians all over the world are under attack from this destructive enemy. He has threatened believers in all times and places and will continue to do so until judgment day. But Christ already defeated him at Calvary. His present assaults are only death throes until his complete annihilation.

In our second focus verse, Peter reminds Christians that all their sufferings, even the devil's devastating attacks, are only for a little while. Paul assures us of much the same thing when he says that our present afflictions are light and momentary compared to the incomparable weight of our future glory (2 Cor. 4:17).

It often seems as if our troubles will never end. Grief over a wayward child drags on for years. The pain of being abandoned by a parent or spouse never really goes away. The fight against deeply embedded sin remains acute. But these are all present distresses that last only a little while compared to our future glory.

Before we know it, Christ will return. God will perfect, establish, strengthen, and settle believers. Their minds and bodies will be faultless and fully restored with their souls. God already establishes the foundation of our faith that will never be moved. He daily confirms and strengthens our faith to each task He places before us. Our glorious future is sure. It will be accomplished through the work of the God of all grace, who calls us to His eternal glory in Christ (v. 10).

To God alone be glory and dominion forever and ever! Peace to all of you who are in Christ. Amen (vv. 11, 14).

Questions for Reflection

How does the placement of verse 7 change the way I view it?

What cares in my grip need to be handed over to the Lord so that I can rest in Him?

In what specific ways can I show today that I understand my suffering is temporary?

31

RIGHTFUL REST

Read: Revelation 21–22

And I heard a voice from heaven saying unto me, Write, Blessed are the dead which die in the Lord from henceforth: Yea, saith the Spirit, that they may rest from their labours; and their works do follow them.
—REVELATION 14:13

Blessed are they that do his commandments, that they may have right to the tree of life, and may enter in through the gates into the city.
—REVELATION 22:14

Throughout this last month, we've looked at key Scripture texts that affirm God's creation ordinance for Sabbath rest, confirm the biblical command for daily rest, and anticipate the guaranteed promise of eternal rest.

Few passages convey as much hope for eternal rest as the final chapters in the book of Revelation. Although I've read these passages many times, tears still fill my eyes at each reading. Beautiful images portray the peaceful future God guarantees believers.

Revelation 14:13 tells us that those who die in the Lord will rest from their labors. It also tells us that our work will follow us. We don't understand exactly how this will be, but it brings to mind that familiar quote from a poem by missionary C. T. Studd: "Only one life, t'will soon be past, Only what's done for Christ will last."

Our homes, money, fame, or other worldly successes will not follow us to heaven. Self-righteous endeavors performed in a spirit of pious religiosity will remain behind. Nothing will follow us into our eternal rest except kingdom efforts, sacrificially offered with servant hearts that deny self-promotion and seek only God's glory.

Revelation 21 paints a vivid depiction of eternal rest. The sea, which biblically symbolizes rebellious nations, will no longer surge over coastal lands to drown thousands of people in destructive tsunamis. The holy city, the church of Christ, will arrive like a pure bride adorned in pearls and lace for her husband. God will dwell with His people even more intimately than when Christ first came as Emmanuel, God with us.

Our heavenly Father will wrap His arms around us and wipe each tear from our eyes. Death will die. Sorrow will flee. Crying will cease. Pain will perish. All our present trials will become the "former things" (Rev. 21:4) that no longer exist.

For the first time, we will really live. We will dwell securely in a dazzling city that is beautiful beyond imagination, entering through the Old Testament gates of Israel's twelve tribes and resting on the New Testament foundations of Christ's twelve apostles. Just as God created light before He created the sun and moon in the beginning, He Himself will provide light with no sun or moon when all things begin anew. The gates of this glorious city will never close because no enemy will attack and no night will fall. No evil person, thing, or spirit will ever enter through these open gates, only those whose names are written in the Lamb's Book of Life.

As we read Revelation 22, it seems we walk beside the apostle John as the angel escorts him into the city. He eloquently describes its amazing sights as well as the emotions experienced and promises conveyed:

> And he shewed me a pure river of water of life, clear as crystal, proceeding out of the throne of God and of the Lamb. In the midst of the street of it, and on either side of the river, was there the tree of life, which bare twelve manner of fruits, and yielded her fruit every month: and the leaves of the tree were for the healing of the nations. And there shall be no more curse: but the throne of God and of the Lamb shall be in it; and his servants shall serve him: and they shall see his face; and his name shall be in their foreheads. And there shall be no night there; and they need no candle, neither light of the sun; for the Lord God giveth them light: and they shall reign for ever and ever (vv. 1–5).

From the throne of God and the Lamb flows a crystal clear river of rejuvenating water. Beside the river stands the Tree of Life, bearing monthly fruit and sprouting healing leaves. All the effects of the curse will disappear. We will see God's face and carry His name continually before us in our minds and bodies. We will no longer need artificial light to dispel the darkness of night or even open shades to let the sun shine into our dim homes. For the Lord will be our light. In His eternal light and great mercy, we will reign with Him forever.

As we live now in these shadowlands, we are blessed when we keep God's commands and worship only Him.

When Christ returns, He will reward us according to what we have done with our lives. Revelation 22:14 tells us that believers will have the right to the Tree of Life and may enter through the gates into the city.

Christ has done all that was necessary to earn our salvation. His perfect life, His substitutionary death, His powerful resurrection, and His sovereign ascension guarantee our entrance into the heavenly city. Christ paid the total entrance price. Our salvation depends in no way on anything we have done.

Ephesians 2:8–9 says, "For by grace are ye saved through faith; and that not of yourselves: it is the gift of God: not of works, lest any man should boast." Salvation is a free gift of God, totally by grace through faith. We can't boast in our works, the best of which are like filthy rags (Isa. 64:6). In question and answer 63, the Heidelberg Catechism asks, "How can you say that the good we do doesn't earn anything when God promises to reward it in this life and the next?" It answers, "This reward is not earned; it is a gift of grace." Salvation is a gift of God's grace through faith, from first to last (Rom. 1:17). But those who have been saved through Christ's atoning and effective work are called to obey God. And true believers will want to show their gratitude to God for His amazing grace and marvelous salvation.

Only those regenerated by the Spirit may enter into eternal rest. They alone may dwell with the root and offspring of David, the bright and morning star. They alone may freely drink the water of life. They alone will experience the rest God grants to His dearly beloved children through the abundant grace of our Lord Jesus Christ. Amen.

Questions for Reflection

How do God's promises for eternal rest comfort me today?

How does this vision of future rest affect the way I will live today?

How can I continue to rest in the Lord every day and every month of every year?